IN THE DARK ROOM

Brian Dillon was born in Dublin in 1969. His books include *Suppose a Sentence, Essayism, The Great Explosion* (shortlisted for the Ondaatje Prize), *Objects in This Mirror: Essays, I Am Sitting in a Room, Sanctuary, Tormented Hope: Nine Hypochondriac Lives* (shortlisted for the Wellcome Book Prize) and *In the Dark Room*, which won the Irish Book Award for non-fiction. His writing has appeared in the *Guardian, New York Times, London Review of Books*, the *New Yorker, New York Review of Books, frieze* and *Artforum*. He has curated exhibitions for Tate and Hayward galleries. He lives in London.

Frances Wilson is a biographer, whose books include *The Ballad of Dorothy Wordsworth* and *Guilty Thing: A Life of Thomas De Quincey*. She teaches writing at Goldsmiths College, University of London.

'*In the Dark Room* moves beyond the specificity of recollected grief to explore the history of attempts to understand memory, from De Quincey to Proust and Bachelard. Like Van Veen in Nabokov's *Ada or Ardor*, Dillon delights in the texture of time, "in its stuff and spread, in the fall of its folds". The personal blends effortlessly with the universal to form a deeply evocative meditation on loss and the passage of time.'
— P. D. Smith, *Guardian*

'It is the deeply emotive nature of his "journey into memory" that presents Dillon with such a formidable task. Yet he not only succeeds in translating his personal experience into a book of immense, disturbingly lucid insight, but in doing so has written a meditation on the nature of memory that, in many places, could compare to the most open-hearted writings of Roland Barthes. It is an amazing achievement in terms of prose style alone.'
— Michael Bracewell, *Daily Telegraph*

'There are plenty of memoirs of unhappy childhoods on our shelves. Few of them, though, have the intelligence or rigour of this first book by critic Brian Dillon, which is less a personal narrative than an anguished monument to the idea of memory itself. ... Of all the cultural heavyweights he calls as witness (such as Barthes, Benjamin and Sebald), none fits Dillon's book better than Rachel Whiteread. His home was as filled with silence, sulky, embarrassed and pained, as was her "House" with miraculously solidified space. *In the Dark Room* is an equally impressive achievement.'
— Jonathan Gibbs, *Independent*

Fitzcarraldo Editions

IN THE DARK ROOM

BRIAN DILLON

FOREWORD

In the Dark Room, originally published in 2005, is a meditation on mourning and an excavation of memory. It was also Brian Dillon's first book, and we might see it as the prelude to his subsequent essays on photography and hypochondria, artists and ruins, essayists and what he calls 'essayism'. How, Dillon asks, does memory – that 'refined and slow-drying medium which covers everything' – adhere to ashtrays and snow globes, stairwells and hallways? The answer is explored through the catastrophe of his family life.

When he was fifteen, Dillon's mother died of a rare autoimmune disorder and five years later his father suffered a fatal heart attack. 'The double bulwark' of his parents' deaths creates what Dillon describes as 'a storehouse of memories all the more alluring for being glimpsed through the thick portal of mourning'. The world he returns to in these pages is 'submerged', settled in a 'strange submarine resting place', as though the objects and images contained here 'could not survive in the corrosive air of a clear recollection'. In his *Philosophical Enquiry into the Origin of our Ideas of the Sublime and Beautiful*, Edmund Burke observed how 'it is in the nature of grief to keep its object perpetually in its eye ... to repeat all the circumstances that attend to it'. Dillon attends, with unflinching intensity, to the objects and circumstances of his grief, the ferocity of his intellect holding in check the seductions of elegy.

The book begins in 1993 with Dillon, aged twenty-four, leaving for the last time the semi-detached in Dublin where he and his brothers were born. The house is now empty, and 'no house could be more comprehensively stocked with the detritus of the past than the empty house'. Many of Dillon's memories are of last times: the last family holiday, his last look at his mother's face, his last look at his father's body, the last argument he had with his brothers. Hypochondria, from which he suffered, is equally focused on finality. 'Nothing of the everyday,' Dillon explains of the gain from his condition, 'can match the exhilaration of rebirth that seizes one when the imagined disorder fails to become real'. For that brief moment, he is not living in end time.

To guide him through the valley of shades, Dillon is accompanied by Roland Barthes, Jorge Luis Borges, Charles Baudelaire, John Berger, Gaston Bachelard, Henri Bergson, and Walter Benjamin. His mind is cultivated in the soil of the twentieth century but seeded in British Romanticism – at least in Borges's understanding of Romanticism as 'a feeling of loss'. Barthes's *Camera Lucida* and Proust's *À la recherche du temps perdu* are the acknowledged precursors to *In the Dark Room*, but it is as a late Romantic that I read Brian Dillon. The high austerity of his project, the concern with ruins and the growth of his own mind, the return to childhood, the intimations of mortality all recall Wordsworth, who was also orphaned before he reached adulthood, whose writing was also born of loss. In *The Prelude* Wordsworth described himself as 'conscious of myself / And of some other being' and this double consciousness is what Dillon also attends to in these pages, where he is both narrator and subject, patient and doctor, adult and child (the older Dillon has no sympathy for his younger self). He is moreover – and this is the most striking aspect of his prose – vigilantly present as a seeing eye and curiously absent as an ego. Dillon, who notices everything, is alert to his own disappearance: looking at photographs of his younger self, taken before the death of his mother, he sees in his form a solidity that has since vanished; he has 'evanesced' through grief, to the point where he would now, he fears, fail to even register on film. But if Dillon is continually disappearing, he reappears in the bodies of his parents. In a photograph of his father aged seven, Dillon sees, 'as if hovering below the surface', his own unborn self. In appearance he is his father's double, his living shade. After his mother's death, Dillon's skin began to stiffen, bristle and burn in a mirroring of her own horrific symptoms. Bodies, he notes, remember in their own way.

Dillon describes memory as 'a sort of space, in which

are piled up ... all manner of essential or useless objects'. He places these objects – pipes, pens, Bibles, churches and corner cabinets – in five chapters called 'House', 'Things', 'Photographs', 'Bodies' and 'Places'. Dillon's titles, like labels on boxes to be stored in the attic, describe his method: he accumulates, and then categorizes, chaos. He also freely associates, allowing one thing to lead him to another. In 'House' Dillon recalls Thomas De Quincey's description, in *Confessions of an English Opium Eater*, of the auditory effect of the Whispering Gallery beneath the dome at St Paul's Cathedral: 'a word or question uttered at one end ... in the gentlest of whispers, is reverberated at the other in peals of thunder'. For De Quincey, and also for Dillon, the progress of the whisper is a metaphor for memory: what at the start of a life seems of little impact speaks by the end 'in volleying thunders'. In 'Places' Dillon turns to George Eliot's description, in *Middlemarch*, of Dorothea Brooke's honeymoon in Rome, where she wanders alone through St Peter's. What 'accosted' him in the passage, Dillon recalls, 'is Eliot's insistence on the way in which the interior of the church persists in Dorothea's imagination', and he now returns to the vast, Victorian monument in which the funerals of his parents took place. As a child he had once fainted here during family mass, and the church is as frightening as the hospital in which his mother is treated. Like one of Piranesi's prisons, the church became 'a void into which I used to feel I might fall: I would gaze, in distracted moments, at its upper reaches, and wonder what it would be like to drift towards the distant ceiling and hang there, looking down on the congregation below.' This suspended position, high in the vaults and looking down, is where Dillon can often be found. It is only when he confronts the consolations of Catholicism that his tone – always taut, occasionally tense – turns to rancorous anger. His father's funeral 'had exposed our ancient family secret: our affinity with this monstrous architecture, this unbearable weight of solid silence and droning piety, these poisonous clouds of incense and candle smoke'.

The dark room, where photographic negatives are developed into images, is Dillon's central metaphor for memory. But the darkness he inhabits is occasionally illuminated by a lighthouse beam. In one such instance it is early morning; he is in bed, his mother is in hospital and his father, having just come off the telephone, is standing in the doorway speaking to him. 'And the phrase which joins the feeble light from the doorway to the shaft of sunlight from behind the curtains at the other corner of the room is "She doesn't have long."' Dillon has many devastating sentences, but this is the one I cannot forget, that wounds me like the punctum of a photograph. He continues:

> To wake in the night and find that the light from the opening above my bedroom door was once again stretched across the ceiling was in later years my greatest nocturnal fear. Like the lamp of a lighthouse which no longer turns but is stuck in a single, cyclopean beam of panic, it signalled a danger which would instantly be confirmed by a hushed voice or a footfall on the landing.

Dillon's prose also stores memories, and contained in this scene is the footfall of another. When, in *To the Lighthouse*, Mrs Ramsey dies and the holiday house is abandoned, 'certain airs ... ventured indoors ... Some random light directing them with its pale footfall upon stair and mat, from some uncovered star, or wandering ship, or the Lighthouse even.' De Quincey too, Dillon notes, associated death with light coming through a bedroom window, and he also mapped his grief onto the architectural spaces of the childhood home.

Wordsworth, De Quincey's mentor, might have called Dillon's 'cyclopean beam of panic' a 'spot of time', one of those moments of imaginative convergence – like a naked pool, or a woman with a basket on her head – that penetrates the mind. The spot of time that contains the death of Dillon's mother anticipates another spot of time, in the section called 'Waiting Room'. Once again lying on his bed, Dillon is now told by his brother, standing at the door, that their father has died: 'My father is dead. No, my mother is dead (I know because I was here: I lay here, in this room, on this bed, the morning after she died). But my father is dead too.' The reality of his loss is figured in the emptiness of the hall at the bottom of the stairs: 'For the briefest moment, that space might have contained anything at all; the possibility of a grotesque mistake, of a violent or lingering death, or time turning away from the course to which I am trying to accommodate myself.' Hovering below the surface of these lines is the memory of the young Wordsworth in *The Prelude*, also waiting, also with his brothers, for the horses that will carry him from school to the home in which his father will also soon die.

It is De Quincey who gave us the metaphor of the human brain as a palimpsest, onto which 'everlasting layers of ideas, images, feelings, have fallen ... softly as light. Each succession has seemed to bury all that went before. And yet, in reality, not one has been extinguished.' In Dillon's hands, De Quincey's image converges, like the light from the doorway and the light from behind the curtains, with that of the Whispering Gallery. 'Not only', Dillon writes, 'do the events of the past remain carved into the mind, but it is precisely the tiniest and faintest marks that will one day make their presence felt, magnified to monstrous, grotesque legibility'. It is the slow surfacing of these marks that Dillon makes visible in this extraordinary book, which itself remains carved in the mind.

Frances Wilson, London, 2017

IN THE DARK ROOM

To Pod and Ned, from Bid

'Time which antiquates Antiquities, and hath an art to make dust of all things, hath yet spared these *minor* monuments.'
—— Sir Thomas Browne, *Hydriotaphia*

'This is the time. And this is the record of the time.'
—— Laurie Anderson, 'From the Air'

CONTENTS

HOUSE

'It is only in the burning house that the
fundamental architectural problem becomes
visible for the first time.'
— Giorgio Agamben, 'The Melancholy Angel'

¶ *View by appointment*

The house in question stands at the western end of an almost semicircular road that curves off a wider suburban thoroughfare. Approached from that end, the house remains invisible until one has rounded a long, thickly hedged garden on the left; even then it would not be the first one you noticed, opposite you, in a row of architecturally identical, semi-detached homes. Your eye might be drawn instead by the pristine paintwork of a house a few doors to the right (one of the few to have retained the original look of a 1930s semi); by the newly concreted garden of the house next door; or by the abutting house on the left, with its comic grid of mock-Tudor window frames. The house we are approaching refuses to accost the eye in any way; indeed, it seems to have retreated from the street, to have settled itself a little further back in space and time.

Perhaps one's gaze doesn't settle swiftly on this house because the colour of its pebble-dashed exterior is oddly indeterminate. It is certainly a kind of grey, but a grey so lifeless it barely registers on the retina; it might have been chosen to make the house fade into the clouds above, or to seem a blunt outcrop of the pavement below. The owners of the house could tell you that, when painted a decade ago, it had looked almost tasteful, but the colour (if it is a colour) has faded with shocking rapidity. The structure itself looks as though it has been subject to an alarming erosion, here and there kept at bay by repairs and additions that appear only to have accelerated the decay, to have burdened the house with a weight of optimism it can no longer bear. Atop the wall of the small front garden, a fresh concrete pediment caps a structure that is visibly crumbling on to the pavement outside. By the low iron gate, the slightest pressure on the right-hand pillar will cause it to rock back and forth with a worrying crunch. The pebble-dash is dropping off in chunks, the window sills spalling, the green paint on the front door peeling away to reveal several previous generations of the same green. If you were to risk a knock at the door – if, that is, you had taken the 'For Sale' sign outside as an invitation, and not a warning that something was distinctly amiss here – the mottled chrome handle would doubtless come off in your hand, and if you reached for the doorbell, the resulting toneless rasp would be enough to dispel any thoughts of domestic harmony within. In sum, it's a house that might have been abandoned long ago, or given up, as a concrete franchise on hope, by its inhabitants, left to eke out its last days along with their dwindling prospects. But behind its elderly net curtains (of a colour now indistinguishable from that of the house itself), something is moving: ending and beginning. The house is being transformed, so that before long its interior, which is still full of the stuff of several lives, will start to resemble its sorry exterior, and speak only of what it once was: how it was made out of hopes, plans and dreams that have absconded, leaving their grey shadows behind.

Soon the house will stand empty for the first time in a quarter of a century. Whereas it took years for the façade to reach its current state of decay, the abandonment of the house will have been effected within the space of a week. I am its last tenant. (There will be others, as there have been before; but they are not part of this story, and I can barely credit their existence.) The house will seem to me to rebel against this far too rapid domestic escape act. It has already embarked on a stealthy revenge for the violence inflicted on it in recent days. As if its unfamiliarly echoing rooms have somehow discerned the intensity of hurried shame with which their curators have cleared them of furniture and effects, the house begins to restock itself with ghostly mementoes. Until a few hours ago, the variously sturdy or dishevelled objects that occupied this space had seemed to persist only as temporary reminders of a job to be done and a deadline to be met. But their spectral replacements are already alive with uninvited significance. This house, so swiftly cleansed of all tangible history, suddenly insists on reminding me that something has happened here. The place looks – so I imagine, in a brief fancy I would like to pass off with a wry detachment I can't quite muster – like the scene of a crime. From the corners of my vision, certain blanknesses obtrude: pallid voids lately hidden by ageing furniture and gloomily familiar pictures (these gaps now dustily outlined like improbably proportioned or oddly articulated corpses). Here lurks the evidence of something recently deceased. The absent bodies seem to want to speak, to tell of their long history and rapid demise. But as my gaze falls exhaustedly on patches of strangely vivid carpet and sharply patterned wallpaper, I would rather not listen, and so continue my distracted survey.

It is the autumn of 1993, and I am standing in the sitting room of the house in which I grew up and which, within the hour, I will leave for the last time. I am aching and fuddled from lack of sleep, having spent the previous night frantically trying to dispose of the last solid remnants of a shared life that disintegrated long ago, leaving behind something less than a family and something more than I currently care to acknowledge. My two younger brothers left earlier in the morning. Their departure was a relief: we had argued long into the night about how much of this glum inheritance to leave behind, how much to dump in the skip which has sat in the street outside for several days, and how much to take with us or disperse among the various relatives who have already spirited away some of the most precious things: the few valuable items of furniture, wedding presents, cracked suitcases full of photographs and papers. If I did not come to blows with Paul, the elder of my brothers, it is only because Kevin, the younger, shouted himself hoarse trying to keep us apart, to stop us descending even further into the storm of recrimination and regret that has overtaken us in recent days. Paul moved out months ago, finally defeated by the wearying routine of almost daily verbal and sometimes physical violence into which our lives have drifted since our father's sudden death two years earlier.

Standing in this empty room on a grey autumn morning whose light, after I have removed the curtains, hardly penetrates the gloom, I am half convinced that all of this is my fault. The decision to sell the house was mine, and after a good deal of fury, tentative consultation with relatives and, I suppose, some reflection on what our barely adult lives have become, my brothers have acquiesced. I have spent long, desperate hours trying to convince them that it is the only sensible option, given the state of disrepair into which the house has fallen and the need to pay for three university educations. I have not managed to broach my actual motivation. We are freeing ourselves from the constant torment of living in a house that was once a family home and is now a persistent reminder of what we have lost. We never speak of that loss – of our mother's long illness and eventual death in the summer of 1985, or of our more recently deceased father – and so I am somehow content to take the part of the acquisitive older brother, eager to cash in his inheritance. In the face of our unspeakable shared grief, there is comfort in a merely mercenary act, a role that sees me rightly condemned to be the last to look on our empty home and to feel the breath of its gathering phantoms. And so I stand in this room, alternately paralysed by the knowledge of what I am leaving and agitated to the point of panic by the need to excavate as much space around me as possible before my time runs out.

Leaving a house for the last time, we can be tempted into an odd fantasy. We start to see it as a sort of ruin; or rather as a pair of ruins, one of which exists only in our imagination. The other is the real space in which we drift about, disconsolately or impatiently, depending on the circumstances of our leave-taking. Our vision of the house splits in two: we see it as we imagine it once was, and in its present state. The latter image is just a ghost of the former. Leaving the house in which one grew up, the chasm between the two times seems especially deep. But haven't we missed something? What gets repressed, as we prepare to go, is not the space itself, but how it felt to live there. The house is only ever what we make of it, and remake, from day to day: to live in a house means ceaselessly refashioning it, reimagining, forgetting and recollecting a place that never stops changing, even if (as is the case in my own family home) we're rarely tempted to redecorate or rebuild.

The texture of a domestic life is woven out of minute readjustments, fantasies and regrets, none of which quite approaches the grand gesture of leaving; but each is itself a sort of abandonment. The slow time of childhood makes these subtle changes seem all the more dramatic. I remember, as a child, feeling these little pangs of loss: dreaming, for example, of the large double bed I slept in until I was about eight years old. Years later, I could still wake, stretch, and expect not to reach the edges of the mattress. As a child, each time you register a disappearance, you think: this is how the house used to be. You recall the solid circle of a badly scratched and stained coffee table that once stood in the centre of a room (and that has now effectively vanished, though it supports a television in the corner of the room); or the familiar sliding doors of a cabinet that was once mounted above the kitchen table and that now sits, awkwardly upended, by the back door, the undignified repository of stray carrier bags. Even more mobile and fragile artifacts seem weighted with nostalgia once torn from their usual homes. A pile of magazines – of pious import, delivered to our door monthly, and conjuring up a world of sunburned missionaries and their grateful congregations – suggests a whole historical era, cut short when the house was extended and a new kitchen inaugurated a fresh, short-lived attempt at order. Each small adjustment to the world of the house contributes to a kind of domestic archaeology, made, for the child, out of well-worn edges and dusty surfaces.

¶ *Theatre of memory*

The notion of the house as a repository of memory is an ancient one. In the classical 'art of memory', the surest way to remember a speech or a story is mentally to disperse its parts about a real or imaginary house. The method has its mythical origin in a tale told by the great rhetorician Cicero in his manual for speechmakers, *De oratore*. In Thessaly, writes Cicero, a noble man named Scopas employed a poet, Simonides, to recite a lyric poem at a banquet. Scopas demands that the poet praise both himself and the gods Castor and Pollux; Simonides, he says, will receive half his fee from the twin deities themselves. Simonides is briefly called away from the celebration by two men demanding to see him outside (they will turn out to be Castor and Pollux). While he is away, the roof of the banqueting hall collapses, crushing Scopas and his guests. Only Simonides can identify the mangled corpses: he has remembered exactly where each guest was sitting. Thus, says Cicero, the art of memory was born, according to which architecture is the model for well-ordered recollection:

> he inferred that persons desiring to train this faculty must
> select places and form mental images of the things they
> wish to remember and store those images in the places, so
> that the order of the places will preserve the order of the
> things, and the images of the things will denote the things
> themselves, and we shall employ the places and images
> respectively as a wax writing-tablet and the letters
> written on it.

Common sense tells us that memory is itself a sort of space, in which are piled up or squirrelled away all manner of essential or useless objects: the memories which we cherish or should like to lose. But Cicero goes one better, making an image of this 'place' out of an actual architecture.

The classical masters of memory have nothing to say about the relationship between memory and home. They imagine instead an ideal house: if it corresponds to a real one, it is only because the orator has discovered an ideal order there, a succession of niches in which to stash the different elements of the text to be remembered. But the rhetorician, wandering in his head from one room to another, laying down in each the concepts, images or words he wishes to recall, can still teach us something about the way memory deals with a more intimate architecture. Mnemonic theorists, from classical times onwards, expend a good deal of intellectual energy on the question of what it is exactly that one should imagine hidden away in the house of memory: a word or a thing. They conclude for the most part that the technique works best when the mind grasps for an object or a picture rather than a word. Of course, the classical student of memory is more interested in the abstract structure of his imagined house than in its status as a domestic interior. But perhaps he has hit on a crucial aspect of the relationship between houses and memory: the teachers of the art of memory tell us that a well-known house is naturally a better repository of memories than an imagined one. What we recall is the image of the house in all its familiarity, rather than a purely abstract sequence we can replay there in our minds.

What do I remember when I think of a house in which I've lived? More than anything, a sense of what it felt like to move about in that medium. I remember the quality of light in a bedroom at dawn; the sudden acoustic shift that occurred when I opened a bathroom door; the curve near the head of a staircase that was a little too steep to run down and a little too wearying on the way up; the warmth of a kitchen in a house without central heating; a door that nobody, not even your parents, who warned you time and again not to do it, could resist slamming; the knowledge that the house had an attic that you had never actually seen (the tiny hatch was too perilously placed above the staircase) but that, despite all evidence to the contrary, you liked to imagine stocked with the fascinating detritus of past generations which an attic ought to contain; the odd sensation, as you wheeled your bicycle along the narrow passageway at the side of the house, that the building was rooted in concrete, in brick foundations, in earth and rock to which you otherwise gave no thought at all; an electric heater, original to the house, which was built into the bedroom wall, and which, you imagined, would kill you stone dead if you flicked its switch and poked it with a finger even before it had begun to glow. Imagine the house, and you picture a passage from empty space to tangible things, from the feeling of moving in an abstract territory to the shock of rediscovering the objects it contains.

In the house of our memory, we're always present, feeling our way round a physicality we know as well as our own bodies. But to see that house empty, to walk around in it for the last time, is to catch sight of a less tangible image: the ghost of ourselves, wandering from room to room like a bad student of classical rhetoric, failing to find the proper places to deposit his lesson. He's lost his bearings: nothing is in the right place, and all the wrong memories lurk dustily in corners, or tumble from their nooks to fall at his feet, broken reminders of his misplaced perspective.

¶ *Walking and falling*

Alone in the house, my task now is to ensure, in a phrase which intrudes into my consciousness from somewhere between the silence of the room and the murmur of the traffic outside, *that we have not left anything behind*. The room is empty; that much is certain. The last argued-over item of furniture – an old armchair, the frayed corners of which still hid the plywood board that my father inserted years before in an effort to alleviate his back pain – has been consigned to the skip. I could stand in its place, in the centre of the room; I could easily walk from that spot in any direction, into the emptiness that the room has become, and nothing would impede my step. But the space is suddenly so full, so teeming with bodies and things, so strewn with objects, gestures and faces, chaotic with years, that I can hardly breathe. Something has clouded my peripheral vision, pressed in on me from the outskirts of my awareness of the room, so that it is only with the weak remembrance of habit that I can edge my way tentatively towards the door, following, half-consciously, the route I would have taken around the edge of a sofa, skirting outstretched legs and discarded newspapers, making for the refuge of a patch of carpet just inside the room, which now seems, alarmingly, brighter than the windowed side.

I reach the door and step out into the hall with a peculiar mixture of fear and faint pride. Whatever it was that enclosed and overcame me in that empty room, it was merely the effect, I tell myself, of fatigue and a too vivid sense of the drama of my leaving. I am, after all, only acting the part of the orphan taking his final tour of the family home, rehearsing a scene I know to be almost comically freighted with cliché and easy sentiment. There is no need for histrionics here. Nobody is going to congratulate me for a twinge of filial regret, or make of my bereft last turn about the house an epic of grief or pity. But equally, there is nobody here to begrudge me a certain melodramatic cast of mind. I am, I remind myself, 'leaving home', and my unease is nothing but an access of self-consciousness about that resonant phrase, nothing more than my overdeveloped sense of my own bereavement. I'm starring, at last, in my own secret performance of a loss which feels unreal and unbearable at the same time.

The hall is not a place to panic. Compared to the shifting planes and uncertain light of the room I have just left, its darkness and narrowness are reassuring. It is as if I have stepped into the still centre of the house, a place that feels strangely submerged, sunk snugly into the foundations of a building that is otherwise tottering and vertiginous, undermined by so many recent emotional tremors. Here I am able at once to call to mind more distant and serene memories. Perhaps it is my perception that I am standing at the bottom of something, in the well formed between the staircase and the closed sitting-room door, that encourages me to look upwards towards the light from a window just below the head of the stairs. I feel suddenly very small, as if I've been dropped into a sort of ravine which recalls me instantly to my childhood perception of this spot. Of all the spaces of the house, this was the most precipitous: a deep and thrillingly perpendicular shaft dug into the middle of my imaginative world. The stairs turned abruptly up to a landing, the thick, square, white railings of which could be glimpsed by the child standing in the hall. The narrowness of the gap between the edge of the landing and the bannisters below – a distance of a few inches, which only properly revealed itself if I looked from directly below or above – made it, in my imagination, a lethal drop: a fantasized crevasse which opened, dizzyingly, out of the white landscape of bannister and staircase.

Into that abyss, I hurled a varied cast of doomed adventurers. Several hapless explorers and reckless Arctic commandos met their ends here. It was the site, too, of more carefully convened experiments. As I feel myself once again dwarfed by the slim column of air above me, I remember that my brothers and I, our curiosity awoken in the pages of a recently acquired encyclopaedia, once emulated Galileo's famous demonstration of the equal velocity of differently weighted descending bodies; we let fall a succession of heavy and light objects from our own imagined sunny balustrade. Our endeavours culminated in imitation of Leonardo da Vinci: we had fashioned, out of straws, paper and tape, a replica of his pyramidal parachute. A tiny plastic soldier had been hung by threads from its four corners, and the fragile ensemble had been launched into the void between the landing and the stairs.

That little figure is falling now, in my dazed imagination, as I stand for the last time in the hallway. But his speed and trajectory are unclear. Should he plummet, lopsided and ungainly, to the floor? Or should he drift out from the stairs to spin slowly and elegantly across the hall, buoyed up for a few amazing seconds above the faded circles of a red and yellow carpet I once imagined dotted with treacherous lakes and quicksands, before coming to rest (executing, in the child's eye, a perfect parachutist's roll) safely at my feet? I can no longer picture the exact fate of our intrepid jumper; my airy and whimsical recollection lands stiffly in the present again. I am faintly embarrassed to find myself likening my orphaned plunge into the thin, uncertain atmosphere of the future to this half-recalled, half-fancied descent. I need to keep moving, to avoid getting tangled in the threads of an unnecessary and lethargic recollection. On no account am I to let my body be caught in attitudes inherited from the life I had led here, or feel myself repeating the gestures of the past: the glance towards the top of the stairs, the swerve around an item of absent furniture. A single look into each room will suffice; there is, after all, nothing to detain me here.

I quicken my pace, dashing to the top of the stairs with the obscure conviction that each room must now be reduced to the platitude of a vacant tableau, a snapshot of an empty stage set. I stop in the doorway of my bedroom and see only its bare floors and naked walls. I refuse to cross to the window or step into the corner where a wardrobe once stood (it lies now at an awkward angle on top of the skip outside). The house, I tell myself, is just a series of empty boxes to be ticked, a stock to be inventoried and shut away. I will remember simply this: the empty house, the evidence of a past finally evacuated of the almost physical presence that overcame me downstairs. I close the doors of the other two bedrooms after only the most cursory glances inside.

I am accumulating images, but keeping my distance from the depths of these rooms, as if the nothingness at their centres might swallow me whole, drag me back into the memories I have finally left behind. At the last moment, I have transformed the space into a safely cartographic set of images which I will take with me to my new home. There, I hope, they will be submerged by new experience, overlain to the point of illegibility. This is the thought that gives me the energy to descend the stairs again, to look briefly into the vacant dining room, to hurry across the kitchen and check that doors and windows are locked, and emerge once more into the hall.

I have closed each door in turn behind me, and the whole house now wraps its silence around me. The only sounds come from the road outside where, very soon, I will take the bags that lie at my feet by the front door. I stand for the last time in the pebbled light from the door's large octagonal window: a form which for years, as I left the house, I briefly reconfigured as six-sided, and just as quickly (for such an alternative seemed unworkably squat and awkward) re-formed into its actual shape, as if summoning an impossibly mutable space out of the lineaments I knew so well. I am seeing now, I imagine, in this final instant before I open the door, the proper outline of the house: a geometry to be measured and forgotten. A shadow moves across the glass, and I know it is time to leave.

¶ *A haunted house*

In the autumn of 2004, a few months after I had begun trying to picture once again my own family home as it stood empty on that morning eleven years earlier, I travelled to see a work of art which I suspected might have something to say about the relationship between houses and memory. The work, by the English artist Tacita Dean, is a film – or rather, three related and subtly different films – entitled *Boots*. On the day in question, I arrived at the Royal Institute of British Architects in London, where the film was to be installed for the next month, to discover that I had mistaken the date of the exhibition's opening: it was not due to begin for another four days. The security guard who informed me of my mistake, however, was sympathetic, and I was directed upstairs to three adjacent rooms, where two technicians were busily preparing a trio of ancient and recalcitrant 16mm projectors. I explained my error, and they agreed that as soon as they had got the first version of the film running (focus was so far proving difficult), I could enter the first darkened room and watch a still slightly shaky back-up print of Dean's film.

Boots is a meditation on architecture and memory, shot in a vast Art Deco villa in Portugal that is now used as exhibition space by a nearby museum. The film takes its title from the nickname of an old family friend of the artist's, so named for his orthopaedic boot, the sound of which, as it strikes the gleaming wooden floors of the villa, echoes through the twenty minutes of the first of the film's three versions. The octogenarian Boots, his frail body supported by two walking sticks, wanders through the house alone, apparently recalling as he goes the building's former, now deceased, inhabitant: a woman, Blanche, with whom, many years ago, he had an affair.

36

In fact, the story he fashions out of the odd muttered reminiscence or sudden exclamation is at least partly fictional. Boots, unscripted, invents his own memories to fill rooms that are brilliantly sunlit and quite empty. He improvises his own character, while Dean's camera gives the house itself a grandly melancholy personality, composed of cool shadows and sudden, blazing expanses of light. As the old man moves through the villa, the viewer realizes that the figure on screen is seeing a quite different film: a series of tableaux made, perhaps, out of his own past, now projected on to the pristine surfaces of an empty house.

I watched Dean's film with a growing sense that I was seeing something very familiar: the moment when one moves through a space both intimately known and at the same time utterly alien. The artist's frail collaborator conjures the most moving images out of the tiniest details of the house: details which, for all the historical resonance of the house itself, and the ravishing cinematography which revives it, were invisible to the viewer. Boots, it seems, is seeing ghosts. 'One has the feeling, or I have the feeling,' he sighs at one point, 'that they are still here, but in another dimension ... and that this whole house is in another dimension ... it's not ... of the moment, if you know what I'm trying to say.' Not only is the house, as Boots negotiates its remarkable rooms, overpopulated by mid-century ghosts, but the space itself seems to have dropped out of history, drifted off (like the massive ocean liner it resembles) into unchartable seas of memory.

As this huge, convoluted theatre of memory opened itself up before me on the screen, I was reminded of another, more tangible artistic reflection on the house as an image of recollection and nostalgia. In 1993, the sculptor Rachel Whiteread made a work simply entitled *House*. The sculpture (if that is what it was: various civic dignitaries rushed to condemn it as an inartistic monstrosity) was a cast of the interior of a Victorian house, 'exhibited' in situ at 135 Grove Road, Bow, East London. Whiteread had garnered a certain amount of celebrity from her previous works, in which the interior volume of a single room was cast in blocks, later reassembled in the gallery to form an eerie white ghost of the original space. *House* was a good deal more ambitious and resonant: an entire phantom building was revealed once the outer shell (which was, after all, the house itself) had been removed and the specially formulated concrete beneath revealed. The sculpture unearthed an impossible volume: the solid replica of an empty interior, the image of a void once enclosed and supported by real bricks, real plaster.

I have never seen Whiteread's *House*: after months of controversy, it was finally demolished, and even the fact that the artist had won that year's Turner Prize could not save it (might, indeed, have hastened its end). But photographs of it suggest that for a time it must have soaked up the memory of its environs: the surrounding streets which, pocked with derelict houses, had eventually been demolished. Stranded at the edge of the empty park that had replaced them, the sculpture gave the impression of having solidified memory itself. This was an illusion: it was not a solid mass at all, but a collection of vacant concrete boxes, held together by an invisible interior armature. You could have broken through its surface – some local squatters attempted to do just this – but you would not have found a habitable space, just a mass of wooden and metal supports. To the viewer on the outside, however, *House* made manifest a feeling that only occasionally overtakes one at home: that the substance of the house – the layers of brick, plaster, paint and wallpaper – is quite unreal, that the true house is the space in which we move. It is the empty volume that we get used to, that makes our bodies move in particular ways, that forms habits and physical attitudes which persist, awkwardly, after we have left.

We often think of nostalgia – which is nothing more or less, etymologically, than the desire for home – as accruing to objects and images (and so it does, as we shall see later). But there is another sort of ache for the past, which has nothing to do with the visible and tangible world and everything to do with the void that abuts it in the most complex ways. If the photographic evidence is to be believed, visitors to Whiteread's *House* must have been startled not only by the obtuse volume of the thing, but also by the way that emptiness was so minutely etched and convoluted. A house is not made of flat surfaces, but of odd protrusions, embossed or striated planes. Each tiny recession of the solid world around us is an extension of our own space, and therefore full of memory: a refined and slow-drying medium which covers everything. Nostalgia is no longer the word to describe the moment when we see the space around us for the complicated void it really is. At that instant – the instant, for me, of seeing the house empty for the first and last time – it becomes properly uncanny (which is to say: *unhomely*). The house no longer looks like itself, and yet it is reduced to its essence for the first time: recognizably a house from which we have been banished. The brilliance of *House* lay in the way it depended for its existence on a specific, unrepresentable space, and at the same time recalled all those who saw it (perhaps especially those who rejected it as art) to the vanished chambers of their own pasts. No house could be more comprehensively stocked with the detritus of the past than the empty house.

¶ *Still life*

The house transforms every remembered incident into an arrangement of bodies in a given space. When I recall what happened in our house – or, at least, as much of it as might compose a narrative of sorts – it seems that what has stayed with me is a collection of snapshots: the space frozen into a series of tableaux. I don't think that the phenomenon is entirely a function of my present distance from the house, from the space which seems to have imposed itself on everything that occurred there, to have mapped our family history according to the co-ordinates of meaning provided by a room, a doorway, an arrangement of furniture or habit of occupying, each of us, particular places at particular times. The sense one often has that a house is something living (we talk of a house *coming to life*, or *settling*) is not wholly fanciful; the house itself had a part in the history I am trying to tell.

The vertigo that overcame me in my final minutes before leaving that house has its origin in a sense that each room is a separate passage into the past. (In her diary, Virginia Woolf makes this link between memory and space; she describes how, behind the present which each of her characters inhabits, a profound 'tunnelling' is going on: an unending excavation of the self.) But numerous chambers of experience come to occupy, bewilderingly, the same space. In my memory, I can stand at a specific spot in the house and feel myself thrust into an endless series of adjacent moments. The house is a Chinese box in which, alarmingly, each newly discovered receptacle is no smaller than those that contained it. It is as if every body that ever moved in a room is jostling for a place at the centre of my recollection, stumbling over others, and themselves, in an effort to claim priority in my memory. But the task of judging which of these figures deserves precedence is quite impossible: they all seem to want to adopt the same poses.

According to one of my earliest memories, my father stands looking out of the kitchen window, sometime in the autumn of 1974. I am five years old, and I am sitting at the table with my mother. To my distress, I have become aware that my father, his back to us, is crying. When I ask my mother why, she replies that he is still upset because my grandmother, his mother, is dead. I have no memory of her death other than this moment; I have to dig out a photograph of her grave to remind myself that she died on 8 August of that year. In fact, I barely remember her at all, except, in an image which I may very well have invented, as a silent presence in the corner of her living room. In the kitchen, my father must have heard me, but he does not turn around. He says nothing, and I am immediately convinced that my question has angered him. I am unsure, however, in my welter of shame and confusion, whether his silence says that I ought to have known the answer to my question, or whether its very utterance is inadmissible. I seem to have excavated a chasm of quiet between the kitchen table and the window. I'm aware for the first time – or so I now surmise from a distance filled with numerous reminiscences of this moment – of a specific sort of mute unease at the centre of this household. The silence is inseparable – then and now – from an arrangement in space.

I can no longer reconstruct the prelude or coda to this scene. I cannot even say with certainty whether it occurred before or after my grandmother's funeral (of which I remember nothing). The image is attached to no chronology other than the immovable evidence of a date (though that date resonates: 1974 being the first year I can say with certainty that I remember; that is, I remember it being 1974, and little else). It connects instead to the kitchen itself, and in particular to a recurring dispersal of bodies within that space. A decade later, my mother sits alone at the same table. She has just returned from a brief shopping trip: an excursion cut short by breathlessness and pain. In recent weeks, her active life has contracted to these occasional, hopeless ventures outside the house, as the illness which for years has been gradually constricting her body takes what will turn out to be its final vicious hold. It is not long since she came back from yet another lengthy stay in hospital, and her efforts to remake a semblance of domestic normality have left her, on this grey morning, racked and stranded in a chair, exhausted by a walk of a few hundred metres. She begins, as so often before, to enumerate the sources of her pain: her bone-deep fatigue, the cruel revolt of her lungs against the air, the excruciating torsion of hands which can no longer hold the bags of shopping she has somehow rescued from her aborted journey. As I listen, standing by the kitchen window and looking out on to an empty garden where I hope something will intrude into my field of vision and release me from my locked posture, I know that the lengthening silences between the descriptions of her symptoms are not only the result of her breathlessness, but a sign that she has started to cry. And if I cannot tear myself from this spot and turn towards her to acknowledge her suffering – a movement which would be so alien, so unthinkably intimate that it would surely thrust us both into an atmosphere even more confusing than that which already hovers like a black fog between us – it is partly because I have become rooted to the memory of my father standing in the same place.

The house, it seems, has a habit of freezing its occupants into familiar attitudes, as if forcing them to sit for a wearying series of family portraits. The body rebels against the pose: the longer it is held, the less able the sitters are to free themselves from it. We are like the subjects of a Victorian studio photographer; an ingenious metallic exoskeleton clamps us into place as we sit through an exposure which can only reveal our agony. Time and again we return to the same patterns and stiff postures. We might even begin to wonder if the house itself has designs on our freedom: why else do we find ourselves trapped in these awful arrangements? If I remember how it felt to move through the house, I recall too how I was periodically crippled by it.

For years, my mother insisted that the house was cursed, that some nameless power hidden in its very substance was responsible for her debilitating depression and the later onset of a disease which, while it wasted her body, nourished that mental torment back into hideous life. As a child, I sensibly sided with my father's dismissal of such thoughts as mere superstition, but secretly wondered whether the house might indeed possess a malign memory of its own. I knew little of its history beyond the fact that it had been built in the 1930s and that when my parents bought it, in 1968, it had still borne the traces of its division into flats. These marks would occasionally resurface in the form of a replastered patch on the wall of the sitting room (where there had once been a sink), or the rusted key to the dining room which I would sometimes try in its lock, imagining the house populated by retiring, somewhat shabby tenants eager to hide their adjacent lives from one another. I can still see them: minor civil servants in tweed and gabardine, pleased to have found a quiet suburb in which almost to forget their distance from rural homes, but unsatisfied, doleful, lacking the charm or imagination to negotiate their way out of their solitude to marriage or emigration. Haunted by these antique phantoms, I would try to imagine what tragedy could have occurred here to convince my mother that the house meant her ill. The most plausible and terrible notion with which I would sometimes thrill myself as I passed from room to room was that somebody must have died here, one of those mysterious flat-dwellers. But the vision refused to resolve itself into a question I could put to my parents.

I know now that the 'curse' my mother referred to emanated not from the submerged history of the house, but from its living walls: from the accumulated residue of a life unfolding into chaos and fear at the same time as it became imprisoned in this space which never seemed to change. Apart from the upheaval of an extension to the kitchen when I was twelve, all my parents' attempts to redecorate the house resulted, oddly, in the reinstatement of the same glum decor. Wallpapers seemed, no matter how new, to be sodden through with the pattern of the old; my bedroom's eccentric combination of sky-blue walls and mud-brown carpet was stripped and substituted with a more vivid, less attractive simulacrum of the same scheme. For my mother, the house must have become, as it would eventually for me, too laden with years: the years of her struggle with depression, the years of uncertainty as the diagnosis of a rare autoimmune disorder gave way to ever more alarming, though not yet crippling, symptoms. And finally: the years of an at last solid and unremitting pain, of a desperate effort to accommodate her failing body to the demands of the space around her, to cook, wash or even sleep without the physical world turning on her, harsh and exigent.

> To those who have never visited the Whispering Gallery,
> nor have read any account of it amongst other acoustic
> phenomena described in scientific treatises, it may be
> proper to mention, as the distinguishing feature of the
> case, that a word or question, uttered at one end of the
> gallery in the gentlest of whispers, is reverberated at the
> other end in peals of thunder.

So wrote the great Romantic autobiographer and critic
Thomas De Quincey in 1856, in the revised version of
his *Confessions of an English Opium-Eater*, originally published in 1821. Beneath the dome of St Paul's Cathedral
in London, this peculiar auditory phenomenon is said to
startle visitors standing at opposite ends of the gallery.
It is nowadays untestable to the general public, whose
massed presence deadens the air and ensures that they
will never encounter the ghostly voice that De Quincey
claims to have heard. He seems, anyway, to have vastly
exaggerated the volume of his interlocutor: a boyhood
friend who stood, in 1800, at one end of the Whispering
Gallery, 'breathing in the softest of whispers a solemn
but not acceptable truth' that 'reached me as a deafening
menace in tempestuous uproars'. De Quincey doesn't
tell us what the 'solemn truth' was; the point of the anecdote is in the image of the gallery itself, which provides
him with a resounding metaphor for his own memory.
Two years later, sitting in his Manchester Grammar
School study, aged seventeen, looking for the last time
at his chair, hearth, writing table 'and other familiar
objects', he resolves to run away to London. At that moment, he recalls the Whispering Gallery, and it seems
like a warning: his leaving will echo, in later years, like

an uncannily amplified voice from the past:

> And now, in these last lingering moments, when I
> dreamed ominously with open eyes in my Manchester
> study, once again that London menace broke angrily upon
> me as out of a thick cloud with redoubled strength; a voice,
> too late for warning, seemed audibly to say, 'Once leave
> this house, and a Rubicon is placed between thee and all
> possibility of return. Thou wilt not say that what thou
> doest is altogether approved in thy secret heart. Even now
> thy conscience speaks against it in sullen whispers; but at
> the other end of thy long life-gallery that same conscience
> will speak to thee in volleying thunders.

De Quincey was obsessed by the relationship between
memory and space: he frames it first of all in the most
spectacular (and often imaginary) architecture, and later in domestic interiors. Memory, in his most personal
formulation, seems to be governed by the image of a
room: a room which keeps changing but which remains,
terribly, the same. But before he lights on this picture
from his past that is also an allegory of the workings
of his memory, he must first negotiate some outland-
ish spaces of his own contriving. In an extraordinary
passage in his *Confessions*, he recounts the horrors of his
opium addiction. (De Quincey was an addict for almost
all of his adult life: half a century in which he struggled
daily with a drug he spent rather a lot of his writing career announcing that he had conquered.) The chapter is
entitled 'The Pains of Opium', and mostly concerns the
dreadful effects of the drug on his dreams, his imagination and his memory. In his dreams, long-forgotten
incidents from his childhood loom up again, fragments
of the past which, he says, his waking self would not have

been able to recognize. There is, he concludes, 'no such thing as *forgetting* possible to the human mind'. Even more unsettling than these revenant events, however, is the fantasized space out of which they emerge:

> In the early stage of my malady, the splendours of my dreams were indeed chiefly architectural: and I beheld such pomp of cities and palaces as was never yet beheld by the waking eye, unless in the clouds. ... The sense of space, and in the end, the sense of time, were both powerfully affected. Buildings, landscapes &c. were exhibited in proportions so vast as the bodily eye is not fitted to receive. Space swelled, and was amplified to an extent of unutterable infinity. This, however, did not disturb me so much as the vast expansion of time; I sometimes seemed to have lived for seventy or one hundred years in one night; nay, sometimes had feelings representative of a millennium passed in that time.

In the book's sequel, *Suspiria de Profundis* (literally, a sigh from the depths: an exhausted echo of the intoxicated voice that speaks in the *Confessions*), De Quincey discovers other, subtler but equally astonishing metaphors for his memory. The human brain, he writes, is a palimpsest: a document endlessly erased and overwritten, but in which the earlier inscriptions can still be deciphered. Not only do the events of the past remain carved into the mind, but it is precisely the tiniest and faintest marks left there that will one day make their presence felt, magnified to monstrous, grotesque legibility. The first part of *Suspiria de Profundis* is called 'The Affliction of Childhood', and the malady in question will turn out, in a sense, to be the pain of memory itself. De Quincey recalls the loss of his young sister when he was six years old. The girl's passing takes its place in a complex Romantic tradition of childhood death scenes: the author is haunted too by the early demise of Wordsworth's daughter Kate, and the poet in turn had fashioned his 'Lucy poems' out of the story of a local child who had perished one night in a snowstorm. What makes De Quincey's narrative so notable in the literature of childhood memory, however, is the way in which everything occurs as if the childhood home itself constituted a kind of architecture of mourning, the dark geometry of recollected and still keen grief.

The tale culminates in the image of a room which De Quincey has recalled often in the intervening years, time and again rehearsing the arrangement of the bedroom where he first saw the corpse of his sister. 'I imagine', he writes,

> that it was exactly high noon when I reached the chamber door; it was locked, but the key was not taken away. Entering, I closed the door so softly, that, although it opened upon a hall which ascended through all the stories, no echo ran along the silent walls. Then turning round, I saw my sister's face. But the bed had been moved, and the back was now turned. Nothing met my eyes but one large window wide open, through which the sun of midsummer at noonday was showering down torrents of splendour. The weather was dry, the sky was cloudless, the blue depths seemed to express types of infinity; and it was not possible for the eye to behold or for the heart to conceive any symbol more pathetic of life or the glory of life.

What De Quincey remembers, more than anything, is the sensation of a specific space. The image develops like a photograph: the author illuminated between the light from the window and the dark mass of the bed where his sister's body lies.

There are no corpses waiting in the remembered bedroom of my childhood. The bodies, as I hope to discover them later, lie elsewhere, in other rooms, which are nonetheless connected, in the maze of memory, to the space I am now trying to picture. Like De Quincey, it is the light that I remember. The single memory I possess of infantile terror is not at all connected to the several shades of darkness which enclosed my bed at night, but solely to the shock of awakening in the early morning. My grandfather (my mother's father) was visiting, and sleeping in the double bed that was mine for most of my childhood. I was relegated to a small camp bed in the corner of the room, beside a huge wardrobe, from the top of which a plaster statue, the 'Child of Prague', looked down. In the dark, I was comforted by my grandfather's presence, but when I awoke early the following morning the statue stood on the floor by my head: staring, it seemed to me, in bizarre complicity with the creatures of the dreams I had just left behind. The room suddenly became monstrous and mobile, and when I later emerged from my hiding place beneath the bedclothes, to find that the statue had returned to its proper place above me, I was convinced that I must keep quiet about this freakish visitation. It was only years later, while taking the statue down from its dusty perch to pack it away with the contents of the room, that I realized my grandfather must have risen in the night and placed it by my bed. Whether he had done it out of piety or mischief, I was never able to decide.

¶ *Lights out*

One of the consoling pleasures of moving to a new home
– which nowadays one hears routinely compared to the
pain and disarray of a bereavement – is the discovery of
those odd architectural features that suggest the aesthetic eccentricity of our predecessors. Why, we wonder, a
door *there*, or (odder) *no door at all* where a door ought
to be. Peculiar boundaries or openings tend to perplex
us most: they conjure up privacies or intimacies with
which we can no longer identify. The German philosopher Theodor Adorno, in exile in America in the
1940s, wrote that the modern conflation of bathroom
and toilet said a great deal about the loss of a particular
European way of life.

A specific sort of conduit from one room to another
often exercised my childish imagination. Above each of
the three bedroom doors in our house was a small square
aperture, lined with the same white-painted wood as the
doorway. These were also to be found in other houses
of the same vintage on our street, but I have never seen
them anywhere else, and my enquiries have elicited only
blank looks from people who live, or have lived, in similar houses. The gap above my own bedroom door was
intriguing enough to explore regularly. With my back
against one side of the door frame and my feet pressed
hard against the other, I could inch my way upwards and
then, one hand clinging to the dusty surface above me,
haul myself far enough to look through to the landing
on the other side. I was always amazed by what I found
there: the aperture seemed considerably thicker than the
wall itself. What looked from below like a simple gap in
the wall, revealed itself, once I was up there, as a passageway from one discrete part of the house to another.
I fantasized about crawling through this narrow space,

but by the time I was tall enough to brace myself against the doorway, I could barely get my head through the hole.

By day, this box of empty space was a curiosity to be first explored, then put to another use: on the way down, I could hang, a hand on either side, till my arms ached and my fingers began to slip from the rounded edges of the wood. At night, it turned the room into a half-lit place between waking and sleeping. After the light was out in my room, a pale yellow lozenge would remain on the ceiling by the door; a cone of light with its point lopped off stretched from the hole above the door to the wardrobe against the opposite wall. The light meant that my parents had not yet gone to bed. I always hoped to get to sleep before it vanished. While the light persisted, the bedroom still seemed part of the house, tethered to other, brightly lit but invisible rooms, where my parents were quietly and busily putting out a fire or laying the kitchen table for breakfast.

A passage at the beginning of *À la recherche du temps perdu*, in which Proust's narrator wakes in bed to find a light still burning outside his room, stages a moment of which my own nocturnal reverie is a pale reflection:

The hour when an invalid, who has been obliged to set out on a journey and to sleep in a strange bed, awakened by a sudden spasm, sees with glad relief a streak of daylight showing under his door. Thank God, it is morning! The servants will be about in a minute: he can ring, and someone will come to look after him. The thought of being assuaged gives him strength to endure his pain. He is certain he heard footsteps: they come nearer, and then die away. The ray of light beneath his door is extinguished. It is midnight; someone has just turned down the gas; the last servant has gone to bed, and he must lie all night in agony with no one to bring him relief.

To wake in the night and find that the light from the opening above my bedroom door was once again stretched across the ceiling was in later years my greatest nocturnal fear. Like the lamp of a lighthouse which no longer turns but is stuck in a single, cyclopean beam of panic, it signalled a danger which would instantly be confirmed by a hushed voice or a footfall on the landing. The light could only denote an emergency, and it was just a matter of time before the door opened and my father would inform us of its full extent. On those nights, my brother and I would lie silent, waiting for the light to go out again. In the morning, I sometimes discovered that it still shone, dimly, through the morning light, though more often than not my father would have turned it off on returning from the hospital where he had left my mother sleeping at last. Perhaps my memory of that faint relic of the night before is related to those mornings when my father had not returned. Having accompanied my mother in an ambulance in the night, he would not get back until evening, and instead his sister, summoned by a phone call in the early hours, opened the bedroom door to rouse us for school.

My memories grow unnervingly brighter: the room blanches into the light of summer, stripped of the consolation of darkness as I wake on a July morning in 1985. My father is at the door. He has not yet said anything, but I already know what is coming. I have been dimly aware, a few minutes earlier, of the sound of a ringing telephone, but my drowsy mind still hopes it was not the telephone but the alarm clock by my bed. My father doesn't move from the doorway, but stands there looking as if at any moment he might express his usual exasperation at two teenage boys reluctant to stir from their beds. But when he speaks, he says something about a hospital. And the phrase which joins the feeble light from the doorway to the shaft of sunlight from behind the curtains at the other corner of the room is: 'She doesn't have long.' The curtains remain closed as Paul and I dress hurriedly and step out into the light of the landing. Downstairs, a taxi is already waiting.

¶ *Waiting room*

The morning after my mother died, I walked the five minutes to the nearest newsagent and bought a magazine. It was a Thursday morning in July, and that was what I did on Thursday mornings in the school holidays. I didn't know what else to do. I could not bear to stay in the house, but also (and here is the source of one minor shame) I wanted to read about the events of the previous weekend, when the global spectacle of Live Aid had glimmered in the corner of the living room of the house in Kerry where we had been holidaying when she was taken ill. I watched it, thinking: everybody I know is watching this, and none of them, outside of my family, know that my mother is about to die. Leaving the house (in my memory, there is nobody else there), I dreaded meeting our neighbours, and so looked straight ahead, avoiding a glance into the gardens on either side of the road. Returning, I rushed to my room and lay for hours on the bed, reading. I didn't want to move from that spot. Outside the bedroom, I knew that things were taking their course: my father was making arrangements; my relatives in Kerry were perhaps already on their way to Dublin; in a room, somewhere – still at the hospital? At the funeral home a short walk from the hospital? I had no idea – my mother's body lay waiting for the funeral the following morning. But for those few hours, none of that really impinged: I was alone in a room, for the first time in weeks. The previous day, my brothers and I had been brought from the hospital to an aunt's house, where we had sat on a sofa for the whole afternoon, silent. My memory of that week is made almost entirely of space, not words.

A house changes after somebody has died: there is suddenly too much space. We all know the symptoms of that change. We set an extra place at the table. We leave empty for months, even years, a chair in which the deceased used to sit. We imagine that at any moment the lost loved one will appear in the room (the air, the light, the whole room would subtly alter). These phenomena are familiar to the point of cliché. So well known, in fact, that, even in the shock of our bereavement, we are surprised (in my case, embarrassed; shame seems to have covered for every other emotion) to find ourselves succumbing to them, as if we feel our grief must, surely, be more original than that. When nothing is said of the absence at the heart of the house, these lapses multiply; if only we could name the emptiness – we do know, after all, its name, her name – we would surely be better able to navigate round it, to keep moving. But time and again we find ourselves stranded in these ludicrous poses, like a photograph from which one figure has been erased: four dummies with nothing to say to one another.

Such is my memory of my home after my mother died. The house seemed to fracture. It no longer enclosed a world, however fraught, but a collection of discrete cells, places where, one would now always be reminded, something had taken place (before, the semblance of a continuum; now, a constellation of vanished moments). In the evenings, I retreated to my bedroom. My brothers started to do the same, until my father, one night, called us back to the sitting room and told us that now, more than ever, was a time to be together, not to wander off on our own. (It was, I think, one of only two moments when he managed to speak to us about what had just happened: the night following my mother's death, as I lay in bed waiting for the light outside to disappear, he had come in to ask us to pray for her.) I think he may have succeeded in dragging us back into an amputated family group for a time, before a routine set in which saw us dispersed about the house again.

Five years later, and the house seems to have been waiting to spring this scene on us again: it is morning, and I have gone to bed late, after taking a day off from university exams. I wake, groggy, to find that Kevin is standing at the bedroom door, and seems to be saying something about the police. (Did he say: 'Something terrible has happened'? How else would you say it? How did he, as he climbed the stairs, begin to formulate that sentence?) Something has happened; but there seems to have been a mistake. He says a name. It is not my father's name. They have got the name wrong. Or they have got the man wrong, the family wrong, the house wrong. It's the wrong day, the wrong city, the wrong country. They've arrived, somehow (and now it starts to seem unlikely, this clerical error back at the station), at entirely the wrong conclusion. That is to say: they have got the wrong dead man, and the wrong place. But my brother seems sure: sure that they have made a mistake, but not the mistake I hope they've made. I imagine my father coming home, through the garden gate, to be told that he's dead: greeting his uniformed visitors in a light tweed suit, as if he knew he'd need to look respectable. My father is dead. No, my *mother* is dead (I know because I was here: I lay here, in this room, on this bed, the morning after she died). But my father is dead too. In a second, I am at the end of the bed, dressing. All I can think is: what do we do now? What exactly are we *supposed* to do now? So I start swearing, as I'm dressing; cursing this morning, this place, right by the window, where I am standing dressing, again, too early in the morning, just like the last time. It is as if time has described a devious spiral and returned me to this point in space, where it will demand of me, again, that I stand here, then go downstairs, where I assume somebody will take me to a hospital, again.

The scene shifts to the hall. At the front door, a man and woman, uniformed, are standing, and I know as soon as I see them that there has been no mistake. The man is holding a small card in a plastic holder (a union card, I think) on which I can clearly recognize my father's signature, and so I listen without objection as they give me the news. My father collapsed, ten minutes from our house, and was dead, of a heart attack, by the time he'd been taken to hospital. Soon, I'm sitting at the kitchen table, and neighbours are making phone calls (to my father's sister, to my mother's sister) and demanding that I drink the glass of whiskey somebody has just set down in front of me. Before long, uncles and aunts have arrived and are making plans to take us to the hospital, to phone the same undertaker who dealt with my mother's funeral. But all I can think of is what has just taken place in the hall: that moment of confusion as I came down the stairs, before seeing the two figures in the doorway, when the future seemed to depend on the empty hall itself. For the briefest moment, that space might have contained anything at all; the possibility of a grotesque mistake, of a violent or lingering death, of time turning away from the course to which I am now trying to accommodate myself.

Three years after my father died, I am standing in the same spot in the hall, waiting to leave. Nothing has changed, except that everything has grown a little shabbier, somehow darker, and smaller. Everything depends once more on this threshold, between the house of the past and what is to come. But by now I am so tired of the house, so sick of its constant shuttling between past and present, so weary of the memories that are everywhere crammed into corners and drifting, untethered, across its floors, that I will gladly leave it to rot. The house, my mother had always insisted, was cursed. But the malediction, it turned out, was mine, and it was retrospective. I had simply never known how much I hated it, till the morning I abandoned it.

¶ *Intimate immensity*

The childhood house, we might say, is a machine for making memories. But the conceit, we must admit, is too crude; for how can we separate what we remember from the space which (to put it again too simply) encloses it? In his classic study of domestic space and imagination, *The Poetics of Space*, the philosopher Gaston Bachelard essays an anatomy of our first home, its organs and members. The house works specifically on our bodies: making them accord with its own interior geometry, encouraging us to move around in it in ways that will stay with us for a lifetime. We remember the house, certainly, but it might be more accurate to say that the house marks us physically:

> But over and beyond our memories, the house we were born in is physically inscribed in us. It is a group of organic habits. After twenty years, in spite of all the other anonymous stairways, we would recapture the reflexes of the 'first stairway', we would not stumble on that rather high step. The house's entire being would open up, faithful to our own being. We would push the door that creaks with the same gesture, we would find our way in the dark to the distant attic. The feel of the tiniest latch has remained in our hands.

Our bodies become used, says Bachelard, to certain spaces. He composes an index of the most meaningful: those secret places in which a child's imagination hides, lost in wonder at the 'intimate immensity' of the house, which is both a whole universe and the tiniest sort of dwelling, a shell in which our earliest reveries take shape. In the furrows and expanses of the house, we uncover for the first time the surfaces on which

60

memory and imagination can be set in motion, safely sliding from room to room, from one plane to another in imitation of thoughts and dreams which will one day occupy much larger and unsettling spaces. The house responds to our most original (and, for Bachelard, universal) urge for a place from which to think, to imagine a cosmos that orbits our intimate nook: 'this house that "clings" to its inhabitant and becomes the cell of a body with its walls close together'. To remember such a place, says Bachelard, is to reconnect with our most solitary sense of ourselves. It is not only the place itself that stays with us, but a capacity for reflection which is forever bound up with the way we moved within it: 'the places in which we have experienced daydreaming reconstitute themselves in a new daydream, and it is because our memories of former dwelling-places are relived as daydreams that these dwelling-places of the past remain in us for all time.'

But the house persists, of course, as something lost, as the image of an intimacy to which we can never return. For all Bachelard's enraptured descriptions of the spaces of childhood – the corners, doorways, cabinets and drawers in which the child finds a paradoxically open field in which to exercise his sense of the imaginative vastness of things – in the end we are banished from this idyllic enclosure and discover ourselves adrift, still tied to its centrifugal centre by the threads of recollection. It is not only a matter of nostalgia, of the longing to return. The desire for home, writes Bachelard, is an urge to fulfil its lost promise:

why were we so quickly sated with the happiness of living in the old house? Why did we not prolong those fleeting hours? In that reality something more than reality was lacking. We did not dream enough in that house. And since it must be recaptured by means of daydreams, liaison is hard to establish. Our memories are encumbered by facts. Beyond the recollections we continually hark back to, we should like to relive our suppressed impressions and the dreams that made us believe in happiness.

The very fact that the house has protected our most unworldly sense of ourselves is what ensures that it now seems utterly lost.

I have the impression that Gaston Bachelard was a happy, if ruminative, child. Everything in his book circles around this vision of childhood daydreaming as a promise of happiness: hours spent sensing oneself at the heart of a universe bordered by the walls of the house, dreaming the rationed space of youth into the plenitude, the open plains, of the future. But while I recognize with Bachelard that the object of childhood memory is exactly this state of reflection, rather than the lucid depiction of datable events, the phenomenon which I am trying to track through the rooms of my childhood is more obscure and closer, perhaps, to that described by the critic Gabriel Josipovici in his book *Touch*. In a chapter devoted to the simple sensation of being in a room, Josipovici sketches the outline of a state of mind that seems to me to grasp much more accurately the child's solitary experience:

> it is the condition of knowing that one is alive but not being able to feel it, of feeling rather that there is life but it is elsewhere and that one is somehow cut off from it. That vague unfocussed longing, which feels as if it would be appeased by the touch of another, is so frustrating precisely because it seems as though so little is required to bring it

to fulfilment, yet that little is nothing less than everything.

It is as if, in the house of my childhood, those moments, which hover somewhere between Bachelard's intimate immensity and Josipovici's bereft ache, have been frozen into tableaux which it is the task of the recollecting adult to breathe on and bring to some warmth of movement and significance. But they seem to want to persist in their icy state, as if their thawing into recognizable events and chronologically articulate histories would set in motion a process of decay which memory has halted. 'In its countless alveoli,' writes Bachelard, 'space contains compressed time. That is what space is for.' Memory is time's frozen breath; locked in the secret spaces of the past like the last breath of an icebound explorer, it records an instant which the historical rescue team, arriving far too late, can only dissipate in legend and surmise: 'to localize memory in time is merely a matter for the biographer and only corresponds to a sort of external history'.

¶ *Subsidence*

In a photograph taken in the spring of 2001, I am standing on the pavement outside the house, for the first time since I left eight years earlier. I have no intention of disturbing the silence of those years by knocking at the door and startling the current inhabitants of the house with my doleful reminiscences of the home which is no longer mine. In the intervening years, I have not only purposely avoided the house itself (I allowed myself no reason to go there) but have in fact steered clear of the whole district, out of a relief to be rid of the memories that still hovered around it (not to speak of those tangible relics that might have accosted me had I had an opportunity to actually go inside), and from a barely acknowledged guilt at having abandoned it in the first place. On the afternoon which this photograph records, it had seemed for the first time a journey which I might make casually, without much of a sense of what it was that I was going back to. It was only later, looking at the snapshot, in which I stood for a few seconds in front of the crumbling wall, that I began to see there something of what I had left behind.

Not much has changed, and yet the house looks dramatically different. The windows have been replaced, the metal frames (which had seemed so modern only a decade before) giving way to apparently sturdier white plastic. So jarring is this addition to the façade, so glaringly at odds with the still decrepit pebble-dash of the walls, that it looks as though the house has been sealed up at all its openings. A new door – with a white plastic frame even thicker than those of the windows – has turned the shallow porch into an airlock between the house and the garden. (In the photograph, I cannot tell if the garden is still there or whether the tarmac, which looks new, now stretches over the whole area in front of the house.) Behind its glass, barely visible above the glare of the camera's inadvertent and unnecessary flash, I can make out the chrome mailbox, from which the door handle has vanished. The handle, I recall, had a habit of jerking loose at one trunnioned end as I pulled the door shut, and it seems that the house's new inhabitants have not worked out how to jam it back into place (or have tired of bending the metal into shape again). Other details have simply vanished: the wrought-iron gate has been removed, leaving the house bereft of the third patch of colour which once brightened its dull frontage. The other two – the front door and an identically green-painted door to the narrow passageway at the side – have conspicuously not been refreshed since I left.

A burglar alarm has been added to the façade of the house. I imagine myself breaking in and wandering through the empty rooms in search of some evidence of my prior presence, some relic to steal from the present and take back to the past. And I remember that a couple of days after my father died, I was woken in the middle of the night by a sound that could only have come from downstairs, at the other side of the house. Somebody was moving about there, stumbling in the dark and trying the handle of the sitting room door. There was enough light in the bedroom to know that Paul was asleep and had heard nothing. But across the landing, I heard Kevin, whose room was directly above the sound of the intruders, moving towards his door. I decided immediately that I would stir from my bed only if I heard a footstep on the stairs, or if Kevin came out on to the landing. Minutes later, a loud crash from the sitting room confirmed that the house was being burgled, and I remember clearly that I thought: they can do what they like, just don't come upstairs. Eventually, I fell back asleep, and had forgotten the whole episode the next morning when I went downstairs to discover the front door open and, in the sitting room, a drawer from a small side table collapsed on the floor. Nothing had been taken, and our burglars (an amateurish lot, I decided, taking advantage of a newspaper death notice, but too stupid, or too reckless, to find out if the house was still inhabited) had clearly panicked when they opened the drawer and it fell, empty, at their feet. But Kevin had lain awake all night, and I realize now that for him the house had altered for ever during that night: from then on, he slept, despite my protestations, with an iron bar beneath his bed.

I am looking now at the photograph I took of a house which was no longer my house. I have never noticed before that from the junction of pavement and tarmac, where there was once a gate on which I was forbidden to swing, there radiates a pattern of cracks that stretches out to the edges of the image. There was a time when I knew every one of these striations, and all the similar scars and contusions that marked my passage towards the house as I turned off the main road and into the quiet curve of ours. I remember now that as I approached the house that day, I remarked how familiar each and every crack still looked, and how at the same time they seemed to have recomposed themselves into a new and startling arrangement: they all led to a house I could no longer enter, a house that in some sense was simply no longer there. The house in the photograph seems to define the centre of a web of memories that have obliterated its actual, concrete presence. It is the meeting place, and the vanishing point, of the lines that make up my perspective on the past. Once, on the morning I prepared to leave it for good, it had seemed to be overpopulated with the shades of the past. I thought I had succeeded, as I closed its door behind me for the last time, in locking those ghosts up once and for all. But in this photograph, with its fractures running from the house to the edges of the frame, it looks as if they have escaped again, and I will have to track their passage elsewhere, in other objects, other spaces, other bodies that have gone wandering in my memory.

THINGS

'Because (in principle) things outlast us, they know
more about us than we know about them: they carry the
experiences they have had with us inside them and are
– in fact – the book of our history opened before us.'
—— W. G. Sebald, *Unrecounted*

'I aspire to the object, to the blessing of matter and
opacity.'
—— E. M. Cioran, *A Short History of Decay*

¶ 'So many things of rarity and observation'

There are, I'm sure, individuals and families for whom the objects they have inherited from deceased loved ones comprise an uninterrupted corridor into the past: historians of the stock of mementoes who consider it their duty to arrange and classify objects with all the dendritic intricacy of a researcher delineating a family tree. But I have never been much impressed by the genealogist's labours. The impulse to trace methodically one's family history through official documents and scraps of correspondence seems as weird to me as the archival fever of those households in which family snapshots are slipped into crackling albums, chronological depositories which assure the viewer of a frictionless unfolding of previous homes, notable occasions and beloved physiognomies. I fail completely to identify with this calm acceptance of time's implacable advance (or with its corollary: the discovery, in words or pictures, of familial secrets, long-forgotten or suppressed scandal). Instead, I have gradually surrounded myself with objects which trace the most random pathways into the past I am now trying to map. I feel myself dispersed, fragmented among these relics, quite unable to fit them into a logical sequence. I can dimly imagine such a story; a whole narrative, properly autobiographical, a chronicle replete with precise dates and an unstoppable propulsion towards the sort of self-knowledge that can conceive of itself as some kind of culmination. These props, in their solid significance, would then furnish the stage of a more vivid and visible drama. But I cannot write it; time and again I bump my faculty of recall against the edges of the things themselves, hopelessly inarticulate reminders of nothing other than their own obtuse persistence.

I wonder if there is not actually a certain pride at work in my abject failure to make of these things a coherent image of the world I would like to remember. It is, after all, the dreadful privilege of the orphan to be able to forget precise chronology (there is nobody there to remind the newly bereaved almost-adult of dates and occasions), and so one invents a universe out of unverifiable impressions and self-serving revisions. Once it has been locked into the prehistory of bereavement, there is a kind of seduction to the memorial fragment: every detail becomes telling, each rescued object a reminder of a vanished era. But I cannot say that these things summon up a story, only that they mark out a space which is immovably still that of their original homes. The double bulwark of my parents' deaths seals a watertight chamber in which to dream everything on the other side of the divide as a storehouse of memories all the more alluring for being glimpsed through the thick portal of mourning. The objects I now attempt to describe are submerged, as if they could not survive in the corrosive air of a clear recollection, and so must be left to drift and settle in their strange submarine resting place, becoming ever more inaccessible as they calcify into myth.

I remember a small plastic snow-globe which used to sit on a shelf in the living room of my grandfather's house in Kerry. It partook of a modest and immediately decipherable narrative: it was a reminder of a place that somebody (my grandfather, my grandmother, or one of their daughters?) had visited. That place has vanished from my memory; I cannot summon the little landscape which the globe enclosed at all, nor the inscription which I am certain was to be read on its base. But the globe still conjures up the objects with which it was surrounded. Its smooth surface was dotted with condensation produced each morning by the competing weather system of the steam from a kettle below. (This was the kettle in which my grandfather, rising early, would delight me with his economical habit of boiling an egg in the water with which he made his tea. Occasionally, disastrous results ensued.) On the wall opposite the shelf where this, my favourite of the house's many ornaments, resided, hung a heavily framed Sacred Heart picture. A yellowing label at the bottom recorded, on a few dotted lines, the names of the family: my grandparents, my mother, her two brothers and three sisters. It also included another child who had died at the age of four, and who had never lived here, though I always imagined my infant uncle playing in the places I did. Between these two poles of the room, a universe of familiar objects expanded around me. At one end a vast, mottled, brown-and-cream-coloured range served for heating and cooking. An electric cooker in the tiny kitchen was a concession to visitors; I don't think my grandfather ever used it. Although I was regularly warned not to approach the range, I was fascinated by its paraphernalia: a collection of thick blackened iron implements for lifting the heavy discs sunk into its top so that a pot could be placed above the fire; a tapered lever of the same heft and hue, used only to prise open the doors on the front; a slim poker with which my mother would stoke the embers. So imposing was the whole edifice that it was always a surprise to see its fiery interior revealed: otherwise, it looked as if it was made of solid iron to its core.

At the other extreme of the living room, everything was cool, fragile and hollow. In one corner was a tall wooden cabinet, painted pale green. A small, meshed rosette of metal set into the door served to ventilate shelves that had once held perishable foodstuffs. Its lower shelves now supported huge, tottering piles of crockery, while on the upper strata I was always surprised, each year, to find jars and bottles left over from the summer before (I think I was half convinced that their contents aged less rapidly in this house than they would have at home). To the right of this cupboard (it was not a cupboard; it was a 'press': the word has only just resurfaced) was a refrigerator that seemed, by its design, to date from the 1950s: a huge object, round-bellied and noisy, which put an end, when I was about ten years old, to the regular trips to my aunt and uncle's nearby house to collect milk, butter and meat. Drinking water, however, was still fetched several times a day in a bucket that inevitably lost a good quarter of its contents as you staggered back along the road.

In my memory, all of this orbits around the colourful interior of the snow-globe. The thing, acquired as a memento, I suppose, of some holiday or pilgrimage, has become a reminder of another world: the universe of my childhood holidays. As I remember it now, its reservoir of fluid seemed gradually to deplete over the years, so that the blizzard which it had once given me such pleasure to set in motion was in later years a shallow and dismal flurry, descending to earth abruptly and surreally (the phenomenon would not be out of place in a Magritte painting) from the empty air above. I could never work out where this watery atmosphere had gone. If it had evaporated, then surely the integrity of this miniature world was threatened, and the entire contents ought to leak away, leaving only a dry residue.

¶ *'Rosebud'*

Objects such as this once mysterious orb are examples of a certain sort of kitsch: that species of miniaturist whimsy inherited from the Victorian obsession with capturing and preserving whole worlds *in nuce*. (The habit was not unrelated to the mid-nineteenth-century discoveries of geologists concerning the age of the earth and its infinitely slow alteration: each household could now watch, fascinated, its own domestic image of evolution.) In her study of the kitsch sensibility, *The Artificial Kingdom*, Celeste Olalquiaga might be describing just such an object when she writes that ornamental orbs 'evoke through visual imagery an intensity of feeling that is otherwise inexpressible: it belongs to the pre-symbolic realm of experience of the unconscious, where events organize and articulate themselves in a non-verbal language sensitive to the most subtle emotional intricacies'.

A few foggy minutes into *Citizen Kane*, one such silent relic becomes the emblem of a long-unspoken pain. Orson Welles whispers the talismanic word which will set the film's elaborate mnemonic machinery into laborious (and, for its first protagonist, the newspaperman who is charged with reconstituting Kane's life, quite fruitless) motion. Keen viewers of the film, attuned to the devious mechanics of Welles's cinematic puzzle, will have spotted (though rarely on a first viewing) the logical oddity of that scene: there is nobody in the room to hear the dying man's last utterance. The entire protracted effort to reassemble the biography of the deceased magnate around this enigmatically enfolded word is in fact a complex delusion, a trick played on the memory of the audience as much as on the endlessly frustrated decoder of the Kane myth. The feint succeeds because

74

the film is not really about words at all (this despite the lengthy narratives – bitter, drunken, self-serving or nostalgic – offered by its reminiscing interviewees) but about things. The little glass snow-globe which falls from Kane's hand as he dies is, by a cunning symbolic sleight, the lens through which, at the end of the film, we see another object: the 'real' Rosebud, the childhood sled which is a reminder of Kane's lost past, now consigned to the flames. The glass memento – pocketed, we remember, after Kane has destroyed the bedroom of his second wife – is a substitute for this other, more tangible reminder, which had already (as the film's closing shot of Kane's prodigious accumulation of useless things reveals) been lost in the museum of his past. The most precious object turns out to be only distantly – that is, poetically, metaphorically – related to the past; it conjures up, in the end, only another object.

One does not need to have acquired such a mad profusion of things as the fictional Charles Foster Kane to be moved by the final image of Welles's film: his deceased hero's treasured plaything ravaged in the furnace of his vast, hubristic home, the varnish on the sled boiling away to reveal, for a second, the beloved name. Nor need we live our lives on quite so melodramatic a scale in order to recognize the secret affinity between the things of our childhoods and their later avatars. Every life is rich with these hidden correspondences between things, submerged collusions between one time and another which are fully expressed only at the moment when one concentrates hard on the object, weighing its presence against other, lost but still imaginable, things. Whole industries exist to convince us of the essential serenity and comfort of such an instant: the warm glow of a memory lovingly caressed. But there is something terrible, too, about the way a dumb artifact can lead us back to the past, if only because its very existence is at odds with the passing of the bodies to which it might once have attached itself, or with which it once shared the space of daily life. That stark contrast makes us fixate too on the objects themselves, as if we can never quite escape the blank obtrusion of dead things into a space, that of personal memory, which we would rather imagine as altogether more fluid and ambiguous.

I have occasionally revolted against the tyranny of the memento, and am sometimes surprised that anything at all has survived my periodic fury at the mere existence of the things around me. The consequent purges have ensured that my stock of childish mementoes (that is, of things I actually owned, as opposed to those objects I have inherited) is pitifully meagre. I can count with certainty only two things. The first is a tiny yellow teddy bear: tissue-stuffed, one-eyed since the Saturday afternoon in the mid-1970s when my father bought it for my brother Paul, who quickly plucked out its right eye and abandoned it. Sewn up and restored to life (which means, in the society of toys, that it was given a name), it survived for years as the diminutive steerer of several cardboard-box buses and trucks, before resting in a bedside locker where, miraculously, it escaped all subsequent redundancy drives. The second object is a decrepit volume of fairy stories by Enid Blyton: an uncharacteristically gruesome collection of moral tales wherein a succession of hapless and gothically illustrated characters are forced to atone for such sins as talking too much and wishing for an endless supply of porridge (the influence of the traditionally ruthless Germanic fairy tale seems to have briefly overtaken the author, but I knew I was safe at least from either of these latter temptations). On the title page, I have inscribed thickly my name and address, followed by the announcement of a generous reward should the book be found and returned to its owner.

I still cannot quite believe that this is the sum total of my hoard, but neither a mental tally of possible hiding places, nor a thorough search through ancient boxes containing numerous relics of later years, will reveal any other object predating the first of several adolescent purges. I remember the excitement of these bouts of destruction, my sense that all of 'that' was at last at an end. In the course of a decade or so, I disposed of toys; books; diaries; drawings; a tiny set of wooden rosary beads given to me on the occasion of my First Communion; a prayer book of the same vintage which contained, I imagined, a photograph of the actual, terrifying moment of transubstantiation (until I realized, years later, as I looked at it for the last time, that the strange fleshly remnant reflected in a chalice was in fact a priest's knuckle); half a dozen penknives of various sizes and degrees of keenness; bits of plastic jewellery spat out by chewing-gum machines (one of which reminded me for months, secretly, of the pale, red-haired daughter of a family who holidayed next door to us three years in a row); a small golden ring into the empty socket of which I had inserted the hand-drawn emblem of my elusive hero, the Scarlet Pimpernel; an alarmingly illuminated toy machine gun which, its twin barrels sparking and wheezing, was, disappointingly, not at all the rugged 'riddler' I longed for one Christmas; a pair of toy binoculars given to me by my paternal grandfather, which, once I had tired of spying on imagined enemies at the bottom of the garden, I had reversed and trained on my room, turning everything I owned into a faraway land, just about to vanish over the horizon.

In an essay on 'The Philosophy of Toys', Charles Baudelaire distinguishes two childish attitudes to playthings: reverence and iconoclasm. There are children for whom the toy is a sort of diminutive deity, a household god to be tended and worshipped, treated with a respect that precludes even touch. The poet warns: 'I would be quick to be on my guard against these *men-children.*' And there are those who cannot tolerate the toy's mystery, who desire immediately, in a frenzy of curiosity, to discover the 'soul' of the thing: 'It is on the more or less swift invasion of this desire that depends the life of a toy. I do not find it in me to blame this infantile mania; it is a first metaphysical tendency.' Perhaps a corresponding typology distinguishes our attitudes to the things of our childhoods once we have begun to think of ourselves as adults. There are individuals who, as the view recedes, institute a kind of private curatorial programme, reminding themselves regularly of the once innocent (now forced, though still pleasurable) import of a particular object. But there are also those of us who see in the collection only an intolerable exigency, a demand for a continuity that is unbearable. I was always ready to plunge the souls of things into perdition.

I must have recognized this tendency in myself at an early age. It was the source, I remember, of some considerable guilt in my teenage years, when I would curse my twelve-year-old self for having recklessly got rid of numerous comic books, notebooks, toy soldiers and a once beloved volume that recounted the adventures, on a stolen motorbike, of mischievous twin penguins, Pen and Gwen. Despite these regrets, I gave in, time and again, to the same impulse to start over, to rid myself of all material ties to the past. When the time came to vacate the family home, I recall, I felt the oppressive air of a whole house full of objects that could not fail, as they were torn from their dusty nooks, to remind me of years which (for years) I had been doing my best to forget. I had now to struggle with my natural urge to bin the lot. I was forced to choose, and in choosing I would ensure that the little I took with me would comprise a new stock of mementoes, their power enhanced by their rarity. There were objects which I was determined would have no place in my new, forgetful life. A large silver crucifix had stood on the dressing table in my bedroom for several years, inherited (morbidly, I now reflected) from an old man with whom my father's father had shared a nursing-home room in the last months of his life, and placed there by my mother. I had immediately loathed the weight it added to my already fretful relationship with the pious objects around me. I turned on it now with a determined spite, waiting until I was alone in the house before unscrewing its heavy base and dismembering the Christ figure. Had I been able, I think I would have torn the sturdy metal of the cross itself to pieces, all the while aware of the essential idiocy of the gesture, but at least assured that this useless reminder of a faith which had saved nobody could no longer follow me on my flight from the house.

Fortunately, a few objects escaped my tearful fury at being reminded of what exactly I was leaving behind. These things are all, I realize, comparatively small: I have hung on to nothing which I could not hold in my hand, cram into a suitcase or neglect on a shelf in plain and unthinking view of my daily life. I cannot pretend that they bear the memorial significance of Charles Foster Kane's fractured ornament, but they are, in some sense, all I have left. In their silent persistence, they call up other objects, other times and places; they attest to the workings of a memory which seems unable to leave them alone, which is forever settling once more on their surfaces. As in those opening moments of *Citizen Kane*, the path through these ghostly things is lit by a fragment of glass.

¶ *Vitrine*

I have just placed on my desk a small glass ashtray that belonged to my father. Already, I have had to remind myself not to use it: just now, searching for the proper words to describe its transparent presence, I slipped, without thinking, a dark hyphen of ash between two radiating prisms of light at its edge, and it occurred to me that of all the objects I still possess from my family home, I have treated this one with the least care. I have never stopped using it, referring to it always as 'my dad's ashtray', as if that title contained no more of the residue of exhausted time than do any of the other private names we give to the everyday objects which surround us. And yet, each time it resurfaces from a cupboard, or newly washed and gleaming, I am a little surprised: first that it has survived for so long without damage, and, more unsettlingly, that it looks so unlike the mental picture of it, in its original home, that I have retained from childhood. The distance between these two objects – one resounding solidly on the desk as I put it back in its place, the other muted by memory – has not altered over the years. It looks no more or less like itself now than it did on the day I took it from the place it had occupied throughout my childhood.

What knowledge can an object preserve? The smooth interior of this thing, which is now a dim reflection of the room in which I am trying to recall its previous life, was once almost invisible to me. It inhabited the right-hand side (my father's side) of my parents' dressing table, where it had all but vanished beneath several of my father's pipes, a selection of workaday bowls and stems from which he would choose one to begin the ritual of cleaning, filling and lighting that so fascinated me. Directly below was a drawer which, as I was occasionally privileged to discover, held other, more elaborate examples. There nestled a bright yellow pipe that appeared to be made of polished bamboo; a short, greyish-white pipe that had a rustic look about it; and a massive, curving and pendulous pipe that I never saw my father smoke, but which I imagined would transform him, uncannily, into the double of the hawk-nosed detective whose image I failed to capture, as I held this pipe to my lips, in the large mirror in the middle of the dressing table.

Both the surface of the table and the drawer below were crammed with a pipe-smoker's paraphernalia: big flat yellow boxes of Swan Vestas, a spider's nest of pipe-cleaners, tobacco tins at various stages of use. I remember the particular pleasure of opening for the first time a large, white-labelled tin and releasing, from beneath a crackling concertina of paper, the fresh, plump smell of new tobacco. The flattened disc would give way slowly under my fingers, freeing itself into cool brown tendrils. These my father would transfer to a bowl lately scraped clean by the blackened blade of a tiny cream-handled knife. The essence of my image of my father clung to this end of the dressing table: a quality captured in the contrast between the hard brown sheen of its top and the mutability of the substances it held. The whole ensemble of objects seemed both intimate and distant, never more so than on the occasion when, as part of my homework, I wrote an essay entitled 'The Day I Smoked My Father's Pipe'. I cannot recall whether this oddly specific, intimate and even transgressive topic was set by a teacher or was my own choice.

The glass ashtray marked the centre of the universe of things which orbited my image of my father. As the years went by, the space around it cleared and the precise spot became more visible. My father smoked less, and eventually gave up completely. The confusion of pipes and pipe-cleaners vanished from the dressing table. When he died, the ashtray was still in its place, now filled with dust rather than ash. I think it may have been in the months following his death – a long summer during which the room where he had slept alone for five years remained undisturbed – that I first paid any close attention to it, and noticed for the first time its true shape.

The object which I had always thought of as a transparent circle was in fact composed of several abutting curves (eight, to be precise; I have just counted them). The interior, I discovered, was completely smooth. The complex explosion of facets which I had imagined on the inside actually fractured the exterior surface, forming a network of diminishing diamonds which pointed to a single, round, lens-like dot at the centre. I vividly recall picking it up one afternoon as I lingered in my parents' room, clearing the dust away and being shocked that an object so familiar to me could suddenly appear so alien. I think it was also at that moment that I first properly discerned that it was identical to another ashtray that had had a more nomadic existence in our household. That one sat often on the kitchen table, tucked to the side of a radio, from which point, on a Sunday afternoon, my father's hand would leave his pipe and pour into a small transparent brown coffee cup a black inch of his Guinness, which I was thrilled to share. The ashtray might then migrate to the sitting room, where a cloud of blue smoke would materialize above my father's head (a fog into which, over the years, I gradually grew). I recalled all of this on that dusty afternoon, and remembered too that I had recently reached for this other ashtray on the morning my father died, relieved to be able to admit I smoked as neighbours and relatives gathered in our bereft house.

It seems to me that this was the instant at which the ashtray stopped being a mere thing and became a memento. It began to suggest a world from which I had recently departed. This was also the moment when it somehow ceased to be itself and started to look and feel unfamiliar, the source of a confusion which perhaps explains why I have kept it near me all these years. It appears to say: the world you think you remember is not as it seems. The recto surface of memory is shadowed, like the glass itself, by its infinitely more complex verso. One side is smooth and reflective, the other jaggedly tactile, composing a nexus of memory images made up of the infinitely detailed patterning of things: a physical realm still sharp and clear beneath the compacted surface of ordinary recollection. The visible landscape of the memento, silted over with nostalgia, conceals the ancient and surprising geology of the object itself.

I have stared long enough at my father's ashtray for it to have disappeared again. It falls back, buried, this time, not beneath the chaos of other objects, but under a pile of memories which cling to it like ancient ash. I have to remind myself of its real weight and shape. I place it, in my imagination, back in its proper home, hearing the sound of glass on wood: a sound that resounds both here and now on the desk in front of me and in a distant recess of my memory. If I were to pick it up and place it carefully down again on the dressing table, it would reflect once more the dark surface, the large brown-spotted mirror and the profusion of my mother's things, inches away in the middle of the space that my parents shared. But to which time does it belong? It is the only object to have survived the desecration of that space and to have remained in my possession. Of course, other objects have absconded elsewhere. I remember a squat jewellery box encrusted with shells. I loved the sound of its lid as it caught a thin lip of wood and felt, for a second, as if it wouldn't close again, before sliding, with a whisper and a tiny pop, back into place. The box was reluctantly related to a decidedly less refined object which sat for years in the sitting room downstairs: a squat wine bottle clumsily decorated, by an aunt of my mother's, with much larger shells and exhibited, I assume, out of a loyalty that precluded aesthetic judgement. The jewellery box was part of a far more delicate arrangement, which included a silver brooch my mother often wore, and which was never condemned to the darkness of the box but always displayed on the shallow glass shelf below the dressing-table mirror. It is already clearly visible in one of the earliest photographs I possess of my mother as an adult.

On top of my mother's bedside table was a modest

collection of books, one of which I still own. When I recall that spot in the room, the small black-bound Bible sits always on top of the pile. It may be that I have fantasized its place at the peak of her little library: the book, before she died, had already acquired a significance which I could hardly bear. The thing itself is unexceptional: encased in fake leather, the rounded corners of which have worn so that they curl, greying, towards the pages whose gilt edges have almost faded away. On those edges corresponding to the New Testament, the gold has been replaced by a pale brown, elongated smudge. I remember how much I resented the presence of this Bible. As my mother's illness worsened, it seemed ever more insistent, a reminder of her increasingly desperate search for some comforting words to assuage her mounting fear. In the last few years of her life, her customary piety had taken a more urgent form. She had joined a local prayer group at our parish church: an offshoot of the Charismatic Movement in which the Catholic Church had seen some hope of reversing the trickle of worshippers away from regular attendance.

If I cannot now separate my unease at this turn in my mother's religious life from my own ordinary and unspoken adolescent rebellion, I can picture clearly the image at which I baulked. My mother's Bible was the symbol of a private agony (and a secret hope) to which I had no access. There was, I remember, another Bible: a much larger, dust-jacketed hardback volume that circulated in our household as the 'family Bible' (it may in fact have had some such title: I recall only its dark blue cover and the paler dust jacket which had a habit of slipping off as soon as it was opened). The black Bible remained wholly hers: I never opened it until she died, and only then did I discover its tattered secrets.

¶ *Transcription*

The scrap of paper has been torn from a spiral-bound notebook: one of the long, slim pads that my mother used for shopping lists, recipes and notes. The lower half of the page has been scissored off. At the bottom of the remaining portion, the blades have diagonally bisected one blue line, leaving a clue, which I almost missed, to the original shape of the page. At the top of the page, my mother has written: '(1 Cor. 13: 4–7)'. Just now, it took me several minutes to decipher what is written beside this initial inscription (I am still a little unsure of the first two words): 'Read as: Thirst change me that I might be always patient, etc.' The text does not accord with the adjacent notation of book, chapter and verse, nor with the reference on the second line: 'Romans 8: 35–9'. The passage from Corinthians, however, is of a piece with the unidentified quotation (if that is what it is); it begins with the words 'Love is patient and kind...' and ends: 'Love bears all things, believes all things, hopes all things, endures all things.' The reference to Romans is specifically to this question: 'Who shall separate us from the love of Christ? Shall tribulation, or distress, or persecution, or famine, or nakedness, or peril, or sword?'

'1 Cor. 13: 4–7': the first numeral is a fat, redoubled bar of ink that replaces a neighbouring, failed effort. I recall very clearly the experience of watching my mother write. I was fascinated by her handwriting (as also by my father's), the elegant product of an educational era for which writing was a kind of ritual, to be undertaken almost for its own sake. I remember that when I was very young my mother's script was always perfectly and modestly decorated, subtle and assured in its regular curves, and I practised for hours to achieve a script as economical and attractive as hers. Even now, after decades of carelessness, I can occasionally catch sight, with a glow of private pleasure, of the brief apparition of her handwriting in my own. It can only be as a result of this juvenile enthusiasm that I recall vividly those moments when she would essay a first mark on the paper, and nothing would appear except a blank furrow. Then, holding the pen at what seemed to me an awkward distance from the writing end, my mother's fingers would fly back and forth in a brief frenzy before a too-thick, overworked line appeared.

> (1 Cor. 13:4-7) ... read as:
> (Romans 8:35-39) "..."
>
> How deep & how high & how wide is gods infinite love for us.

The first line on the slightly yellowed scrap of paper which I am holding now, inches away from my writing hand, conjures that moment precisely. I am almost tempted to fill the empty vertical of her first attempt with a straight 'l', my hand retracing the line she wanted to make. I would like, in fact, to rewrite the whole of this tiny fragment, giving its letters the shapes she must have tried to trace. Because this remnant of my mother's handwriting dates from a period some years after my first enthralment to its bright blue mystery: the writing is still recognizably hers, with its old-fashioned open 'p' and tiny cross for 'and' (a convention to which I have recently reverted after years of clumsily executed ampersands), but something is wrong; her style has contracted, the letters retreating towards the middle of each line, barely venturing above or below. The very texture of the ink has altered, as if applied with slightly too much force by a hand unsure of its ability to maintain a light and uniform line. The words themselves have shrunk; their once languid drift to the right has stiffened; they are not quite perpendicular to the faint tropics of the page, but noticeably more rigid, as if the hand that wrote these words were unsure of making it to the next letter and so has delineated each a little too carefully before moving on. Some letters seem to have stalled completely. The second, upward stroke of a 'w' has clumsily overshot the height of the first, and the letter is now cracked into a pair of badly matched 'v's, utterly uncharacteristic of my mother's serenely flowing hand. Each successive lower-case 'h' is a little less sturdy than the last; the fourth and final example has collapsed, the loop of its back hacked off, the spring of its 'seat' busted. The word 'infinite' has been painfully hobbled: its prefix has come away from the main body of the word, and the third 'i' fails to obscure an 'a', the evidence of a first misspelling.

A single blank line separates the enigmatic pair of biblical references from a complete sentence below. The sentence reads: 'How deep and how high is God's infinite love for us.' I have no idea of the occasion on which she might have written this, nor whether it was a private reminder of a quotation that meant something to her, or a line to be read before others. But the crippled writing is enough to tell me that it dates from that period when her hands had become so twisted and agonized that she held a pen with great difficulty and had to move her whole arm to write. Her fingers could no longer make those minute adjustments which writing demands; it is as if her entire body is twisting and turning to produce these awkward marks.

EPISTLE

A reading from the second letter of St Paul to the Corinthians.

2 Cor. 12:7-10

To keep me from being too elated by the abundance of revelations, a thorn was given me in the flesh, a messenger of Satan, to harass me, to keep me from being too elated. Three times I besought the Lord about this, that it should leave me; but he said to me, 'My grace is sufficient for you, for my power is made perfect in weakness.' I will all the more gladly boast of my weaknesses, that the power of Christ may rest upon me. For the sake of Christ, then, I am content with weaknesses, insults, hardships, persecutions, and calamities; for when I am weak, then I am strong.

My mother's Bible was not part of our family ritual of nightly prayer. It was a private album into which she slipped fragments of prayer, memorial cards and handwritten passages from scripture. They are still there. Among them, another piece of darkening paper has been carefully torn from a missal: a portion of a Sunday Mass, 'a reading from the second letter of St Paul to the Corinthians'. There was a time, after she died and at those rare moments when I examined the contents of the Bible, when I couldn't read this passage without becoming furious at what I thought of as the cruelty of its message. St Paul writes: 'To keep me from being too elated by the abundance of revelations, a thorn was given me in the flesh, a messenger of Satan, to harass me, to keep me from being too elated.' I cannot read this gobbet of theological poison without conjuring the image it must have brought to my mother's mind: her body whole and uncorrupt, open, joyously, to the world around her. And it tortures me still to think that she had to convince herself that she didn't deserve such a life.

I don't recall how this volume made it on to my bookshelves, but I do know that it has sat there for years, mostly undisturbed, occasionally taken down and examined in a rather detached fashion. Beyond my fury at the rigours of a faith with which I cannot identify, I have been wholly unable to connect it to my memory of my mother – until now, when, attending instead to its physical presence, to the book as a thing, I start to see its history come into focus. And I wonder now whether in fact the comfort my mother took from it was less to do with the words she copied out than with that act itself: the calm consolation of writing, even (maybe especially) when the words were not hers. The Bible reminds me, at last, of a familiar image of her: sitting quietly in the evening, copying, more slowly than before, the words that might be her salvation.

¶ *Plethora*

In his extraordinary short story, 'Funes the Memorious', Jorge Luis Borges imagines a memory reduced (or perhaps expanded) to a strict inventory of the myriad physical details which go to make up a life. The story begins, appropriately, with a litany:

> I remember him (I have no right to utter this sacred verb, only one man on earth had that right and he is dead) with a dark passion flower in his hand, seeing it as no one has ever seen it, though he might look at it from the twilight of dawn till that of evening, a whole lifetime. I remember him, with his face taciturn and Indian-like and singularly *remote*, behind the cigarette. I remember (I think) his angular, leather-braiding hands. I remember near those hands a maté gourd bearing the Uruguayan coat of arms; I remember a yellow screen with a vague lake landscape in the window of his house. I clearly remember his voice: the slow, resentful, nasal voice of the old-time dweller of the suburbs, without the Italian sibilants we have today. I never saw him more than three times; the last was in 1887...

The narrator tells us that he had first encountered the appallingly talented Ireneo Funes three years earlier, while out riding with his cousin. The latter had stopped to ask the time of this strange boy, who immediately replied, without a glance at a timepiece or at the sky: 'It's four minutes to eight, young Bernardo Juan Fransisco.' Three years later, the 'chronometrical' Funes has been thrown by a horse and paralysed. His accident seems to have sharpened his already preternatural powers; he now recalls everything with an astonishing clarity. He learns Latin in a matter of days, and astonishes the narrator by memorizing the entirety of Pliny's *Naturalis historia*; when the two meet again, Funes enumerates

> the cases of prodigious memory recorded in the *Naturalis historia*: Cyrus, king of the Persians, who could call every soldier in his armies by name; Mithridates Eupator, who administered the law in the twenty-two languages of his empire; Simonides, inventor of the science of mnemonics; Metrodorus, who practised the art of faithfully repeating what he had heard only once.

Funes's memory outdoes all these classical examples. He can forget nothing: every event, every impression, every fact gleaned from his endless reading and hours spent sitting at his window and staring have been consigned to what he calls the 'garbage heap' of his memory. So accurate is his recall that he rebels against the vagueness of ordinary language and devises a whole new vocabulary to denote numbers: 'In place of seven thousand thirteen, he would say (for example) *Maximo Pérez*; in place of seven thousand, *The Railroad*; other numbers were *Luis Melián Lafinur, Oliman, sulphur, the reins, the whale, the gas, the cauldron, Napoleon, Agustín de Vedia*. In place of five hundred, he would say *nine*.' The absurdity of his system is clear: it demands an impossible renovation of the whole of human speech and thought. The task of enumeration would never be complete: 'he thought that by the hour of his death he would not even have finished classifying all the memories of his childhood.'

Borges's story tells us something about the limits of human memory: a 'perfect' memory would be, in essence, indistinguishable from no memory at all. The unfortunate Funes is forced to remake his world at every moment, in an unending process of pure and pointless accumulation; he is cursed, by his very talent, with 'certain incurable limitations'. By far the most haunting moments in Borges's narrative are those at which the hapless prodigy is transfixed by the horrifying implacability of physical objects: the outline of a cloud, the binding of a book, the foam raised by an oar. 'He was the solitary and lucid spectator', writes Borges, 'of a multiform, instantaneous and almost intolerably precise world.'

In 1970, the American artist and writer Joe Brainard embarked on a project that seems as fraught, and doomed, as that imagined by Borges. In his book *I Remember*, he set out, by means of prefacing each discrete impression with the words of his title, to capture his own past (mostly, his childhood and adolescence) in its most fleeting details. The book (followed by two sequels, *More I Remember* and *More I Remember More*) has the odd effect of rendering each individual recollection a mere frame in the mobile film-strip of the author's memory, and at the same time of investing each fragile moment with significance. It is as if Brainard has written an autobiography with all the narrative drive, all the pretence at continuity and reflection, removed. Like Funes, Brainard seems immune (or so he claims) to overarching ideas; instead, he's obsessed by the texture of things, the child's world of objects and substances which fail to meld into a unified understanding of the world around him. Here he is recalling his covert appropriation of his mother's belongings to his own secret vision:

> I remember a small top drawer full of nylons, and my mother, in a rush, trying to find two that matched.

I remember finding things in that drawer that I wasn't supposed to see, smothered in nylons.

I remember the olive green lining of my mother's olive green "leather" jewellery box, with fold-out trays. When alone in the house, I loved going through it, examining each piece carefully, trying to pick out my favourites. And sometimes, trying something on, but mostly, I just liked to look.

I remember learning very early in life the art of putting back everything exactly the way it was.

In the first volume of Brainard's recollections, there are over one thousand of these entries. While many suggest a historical era – a fifties America of pale green Coca-Cola bottles, high-school yearbooks and clumsy sex – many more are quite devoid of cultural significance (the child, of course, knows nothing of 'culture' anyway; everything simply is what it is). Brainard affects a writerly naivety, as if his impressions are simply the written register of a vacant, unthinking sensibility, dredging from his memory so much useless and insignificant garbage. Of course, as in this brief example, he cannot help grouping his impressions in such a way as to form tantalizing micro-narratives, from which he steps back, as here, to offer laconic commentary on his own past self. Brainard, in the end, is not Funes. But he experiences his project as prodigious, even divine, in its ambition. He writes in a letter to his publisher:

I feel very much like God writing the Bible. I mean, I feel like I am not really writing it but that it is because of me that it is being written. I also feel that it is about everybody else as much as it is about me. And that pleases me. I mean, I feel like I am everybody. And it's a nice feeling. It won't last.

Inspired in part by the examples of Borges and Brainard, the English artist Emma Kay has in recent years produced a body of work that tests the power of her own memory and makes of its inevitable failures an allegory for the generality of human forgetfulness. Kay's most mnemonically ambitious work is *The Bible From Memory*, completed in 1997. Like Joe Brainard, she puts herself in the place of God; she attempts to recount all the events of the Bible in their proper order. Framing her memory of the book as a vast field of text (exhibited as if it were a picture, which in a way it is), she responds to a venerable Christian perspective: the idea that the minutely unfolding history of humanity is glimpsed in the blink of an eye by the watchful deity. But this is also, of course, the believer's fondest desire: a Book so intimately read and recalled that it would float before one's eyes at all times, a constant written reminder, to be quoted or cited at will. At the same time, like the real thing, Kay's Bible is an unruly mass of individual narratives which the printed text tries to amalgamate and control by numbering each fragment.

In Kay's version, which turns the literal word into fugitive stories, the order is untenable. Bits break off and drift about, coming to rest in entirely the wrong place. The Old Testament begins with a passage from the Gospel of St John ('In the beginning was the word') and crucial chronologies get upended: 'David the giant killer was the son of someone famous, and the father of Solomon or the other way around.' The illogic of pure enumeration leads the artist to draw up a new and quite demented catalogue: *The Bible – 2,717 Objects in Order of Appearance* might be an index to the actual book, were it not that its order is unfathomable, and the whole riddled with omissions and repetitions. In Kay's rendering, '1,000 silver shekels' abut meaninglessly against '400 silver shekels': the general category disappears and is replaced by a series of untraceable instances of the same thing. (Of course, as Borges's Funes would insist, there is no such thing as 'the same thing'; each appearance is a separate memory deserving of its own entry in the catalogue.) The list of objects – saddle, stone, stones, another hundred pieces of silver, tent, altar, idols, earrings – tells us everything and nothing. As a way of making sense of the Bible, it is extremely impressive and quite useless.

Any inventory, no matter how thorough, is only ever a partial record of a more chaotic and expansive reality. I know it is fanciful to imagine that I could corral my own past into a comprehensive archive of meaningful artifacts. The real meaning of these few frail objects in front of me lies not in what they tell me about the past, but in their simple and largely accidental survival. It is the fact that they are still with me that matters, and each one deserves to be as carefully mounted and labelled as if it were an example plucked from the richest hoard.

Putting aside my mother's Bible and its contents with a final glance at the still-harrowing state of her handwriting, I have a clear image of the pen she must have used. A blue and silver ballpoint, slimly tapered and clipless (a 'lady's pen'), it always seemed to me a perfectly refined instrument. It was not only the delicate barrel, decorated with a constellation of tiny white stars, that intrigued me, but most of all the mystery of its mechanism. A darker cylinder of blue at the end twisted only very slightly to reveal the point, and I never failed to notice, when the pen appeared from my mother's handbag, that this simple turn, executed with one hand, seemed to set it off from all other, cruder, examples. I coveted it for years, until one Christmas (I was twelve, and already, in the depths of that winter, my mother's frozen hand must have held her pen with slightly less assurance than before) I decided that I wanted one too. The gift required a trip to a shopping centre a few miles away; I hadn't told my mother that I wanted *her* pen exactly, but when we arrived at the stationer's counter, there it was: a green twin to my mother's blue.

I must have put this treasured object aside a few years later, seduced away by a procession of fat-nibbed fountain pens and a little embarrassed to be seen at school sporting such a feminine object (even if I had told myself that the drab green was a more acceptably masculine colour). It was only after both my parents were gone that I took it out again. In the five years between their deaths, I think I might now and then have glimpsed both pens hidden away in drawers and corners, reminders of that December afternoon when I had felt for the first time, returning from our shopping trip, that my mother and I had a new and adult affinity. But this was the kind of thought which, in those years, I would quickly stifle: my mother's belongings stuck around in our household, as quiet and undisturbed as the memory of her to which none of us ever gave a voice. The same silence persisted after my father died. Although his name never interrupted the uneasy truce between the three of us, we found ourselves surrounded by things that insisted on being handled, that made of our daily lives an unspoken conversation with the recent past. My own private response to this gulf between the material endurance of things and the silence that surrounded them was to appropriate, without much thought, certain objects. And so began a brief period, a few years, in which I seem to have gone out of my way to lose as many of my parents' possessions as possible.

I cannot now recall what became of my mother's blue pen. I can only hope that it was spirited away by one of her sisters, who might have recognized in it something of the essence of her. I remember that the green pen was now the one that I identified with her, and carried with me always as a student, along with my father's strapless watch and a gold pen presented to him on some professional occasion. In turn, I managed to lose both pens and break the watch (I can see it now, flying from my hand and landing at the bottom of a college staircase). I remember too my complete despair, standing on a rainy street, ransacking my pockets for the green pen, cursing my foolish urge to keep it about me like a magical talisman whose powers I did not, while I possessed it, yet comprehend.

Only one object remains to me from the chain of interconnected artifacts that I am now recalling. A dusky blue fountain pen with gold detailing and nib: it was hidden, until my father's death, at the back of the top shelf of the wardrobe in my bedroom. I remember, as a child, sometimes happening upon it as I rummaged about there, dragging out an ancient camera, still in its tattered box (I would train its dusty viewfinder on my room before replacing it guiltily). In that darkness, too, was an old vanity case. Its zip yielded reluctantly to reveal a still-gleaming array of mysterious objects: an old-fashioned shaving kit with elaborate, but bladeless, razor; two pristine chrome talc holders; a stiff and unused clothes brush. But it was the pen which I found most compelling, and wholly resistant to my imagination. I could never work out how it functioned. I knew there must be some connection between the tarnished gold of the nib, with its minutely inscribed legend – 'Schaeffer's 33, Made in USA, 14K' – and the svelte rectangle of gold set into its barrel. If I hooked a fingernail under one end, into an oval indentation, the lever would give slightly. But I could never bring myself to pull it back all the way, a movement which might have revealed its purpose. Instead, the pen stayed in an imaginative vacuum: I never asked my father about it, and I wonder now whether he had forgotten about it as it lay snugly and dustily concealed. Eventually, I forgot it too.

After my father died, I dug out his fountain pen and started to use it. Quite why I did so I am unable to say, but it might have had something to do with a sense that the life my brothers and I shared with the remains of our family home was coming to an end, and the pen seemed to connect to a version of my father I found freshly comforting (though I had never seen him use this pen). I quickly discovered that the rubber reservoir into which the pen sucked ink through its nib had perished, and the paltry drop which it was possible to attract was only enough to keep writing for a line or so: about twelve words. It now seems quite bizarre to me that I carried on using it for months in this fashion, refilling it every few minutes. After a few months of this I had the pen repaired, but the fully functioning object quickly lost its allure, and it now sits on my desk as a reminder of a time when its failing machinery was a sort of encouragement, a suggestion that a fresh start to everything was only minutes and inches away, at the tips of my fingers.

¶ *Enigma*

In the corner of our sitting room stood a tall cabinet of dark wood and alarmingly thin and delicately engraved panes – the subject, I seem to recall, of many stern warnings from my mother as I approached. The cabinet contained two bone-china dinner sets: one somewhat garishly edged with gold leaves, the other more elegantly decorated with a subtler and more colourful flora. It was the second set, accompanied by a tentative tinkling, which I was now and then privileged to remove from its glittering home and lay out for a special occasion. For the most part, the contents of the cabinet lay just out of reach, their glassed-in proximity secured by a tiny key which resided in a small pewter vase on the polished surface above. This plane was more accessible, but still a realm from which I was excluded by the preciousness of the objects it supported. A huge crystal vase was flanked by its diminutive siblings. Where the central, gigantic mass ascended to a gaping height, its smaller relations were characterized in my mind by the way their faceted roundness seemed to invite a cool handling. In fact, the flattened prisms which punctuated their surfaces reminded me of nothing so much as the pineapple-shaped hand grenades lobbed, to devastating effect, in the pages of the WWII comic books to which I was addicted. In a rare destructive fantasy, I imagined seizing one of these glassy bomblets and hurling it in the direction of some imagined enemy at the opposite corner of the room.

The contents of this cabinet are now dispersed, safe from my vividly recalled urge to trash the whole delicate armoury. Only one object has survived the slow-motion explosion by which the rest were sent careering into the possession of other family members, an object which had always seemed to inhabit a tactile universe a little closer to my own. 'The blue thing': this is the quite inadequate name by which I used to know a heavy glass bowl that sits on my desk as I write. It had occupied a place just in front of the more precious and transparent glass artifacts. It seemed, even then, to partake of another aesthetic entirely from the gaudy ornaments that surrounded it. Its simple, solid heft felt (and still feels) so much more modern. About three inches high and of a thickness and weight that sits as impressively in my hands now as it did many years ago, its most mysterious attribute was the wide expanse of its rim. The solidity of this thing was only a prelude to the wonder I felt on taking the bowl from its place on the cabinet and gazing down on its surface. For the endlessly alluring sight that greeted me was this: seen from above, the radius of blue which enclosed the darkness at the centre of the bowl held within it a layer of pure gold. This gilt substratum was, and remains, a mystery to me. I turned, as I do now, the glass in my hands, trying to discern where in its depths this vision might reside. It is not there, and my first thought – that it is just the reflection of my own puzzled face – is dispelled as I edge away from the bowl, having placed it on a dark background only to find that the phenomenon persists.

Where some objects connect quite clearly in my memory with real events and circumstances, others recall only themselves. At first, the blue bowl seems one of these: I can link it only to my own past contemplation of it, my state of wonder at its enigmatic colouring. But this is a clue to its real function in my memory. For many years, I have been unable to look at its mutable blue without calling to mind another instance of the same (but of course it is not the same) colour. The image it brings to mind is undated, a fugitive impression from childhood which has stayed with me for I know not what reason. It is the image of a blue enamel saucepan held by my mother in the kitchen of my grandfather's house one summer. The memory amounts to no more than that: a flash of blue at the end of my mother's arm. That blue, which corresponds to no colour I have seen since – and I have looked for it, over the years, everywhere: on the surfaces of things, in the depths of fabric, in a succession of real blue skies and filmed or painted ones – is perfectly visible to me now, and quite incommunicable. It fits no chronology; instead, it simply persists. But the image is not, for all its obscurity, devoid of meaning. It brings with it, as it fades into view in front of the bowl – a cinematographer's match-cut between two rhyming cylinders of blue – a sense of calm, of a chromatic unity of times. The colour seems to have settled into its proper place, to have found its moment, secure in its niche in my memory for precisely the reason it is so mysterious: it is not part of a story.

If that blue recalls anything now, it is, oddly, another colour entirely: the red interior of my mother's sewing box. Here is Walter Benjamin in 1938, in *A Berlin Childhood around 1900*, contemplating the dark interior of his own mother's sewing box:

> I began to question whether the box was really meant
> for sewing in the first place. That the spools of thread
> and yarn within it tormented me by their shady allure
> only strengthened my doubt. What attracted me about
> those spools was their hollow core; originally, this was
> intended for an axle which, on being rotated, would wind
> up the thread on the spool. Now, however, this cavity
> was covered on both sides by a black label which bore,

embossed in gold, the name and number of the firm. Too
great was the temptation to press my fingertips against the
centre of the tag; too intimate, the satisfaction when it tore
and I dipped into the hole beneath.

Benjamin remembers intimacy, depth: a hollow which
promises the dark, vaguely erotic pleasure of probing,
then penetrating, its contents. The sewing box is an
image of concealment and revelation. I remember the
mystery of threads and fabrics, of slipping my fingers
between tattered pattern books to discover ancient
remnants, buttons and needles. But what I recall most
clearly is the sight of the box lying open, the plush red
(which may have been silk) attached to the inside of its
wicker lid thrust back, slightly askew where one hinge
had begun to give way. I remember the box as something
open and alive with activity, moments, to borrow
Benjamin's words, 'when the sewing things ruled over
me with inexorable power' as I submitted to the fittings
and alterations which would stretch an afternoon into
an agony of stillness, boredom and frustration. I do
not remember my mother's increasing discomfort in
later years, as her hands stiffened and she found herself
unable to thread a needle or to force it, with the hardened
but raw tip of her finger, through the fabric. I remember
only that the sewing box was opened less frequently, that
its contents, which once saw a succession of new, bright
objects pass through it on the way to becoming garments
or mendings, now rarely altered, so that already, long
before she died, it seemed a thing from another time, a
memory of childhood while I was still a child.

¶ *Library*

I have around me, scattered on shelves, in chaotic piles, lost in ostensibly temporary storage, about half of the one thousand or so books which my father owned. His library is both an ever-present reminder and a solid embodiment of the ways in which I have tried to give a pattern to his memory. There was a time, I remember, when I endeavoured to keep my father's books together, to maintain the integrity of a collection that had been such a vivid presence in my childhood. But my heart was never in the task of keeping all his years of reading unified on my own bookshelves; the books are now so completely integrated with my own that I sometimes forget whether a given volume is his or my own.

The novelist Georges Perec, in an essay with the playfully prim title 'Brief Notes on the Art and Manner of Arranging One's Books', begins his reflection on his own library by remarking: 'every library answers a twofold need, which is often also a twofold obsession: that of conserving certain objects (books) and that of organizing them in certain ways'. Looking at my father's books, dispersed among my own, I notice that I have belatedly inherited his principle of organization; or rather, have abandoned, as he did in our book-strewn home, any pretence at an order other than that imposed by day-to-day reading habits and the space available. There was a time in my life, not long after my father died, when I subjected both our libraries to a rigorously alphabetical arrangement. Numerous relocations, countless packings and unpackings, have put paid to that project and I realize that I have lately begun to reproduce exactly the unruliness of my father's library: a chaos in which, like him, I insist that I can find my way, that I remember (of course, it is a lie) where each and every volume is. Perec elaborates:

> Books are not dispersed but assembled. Just as we put
> all the pots of jam into a jam cupboard, so we put all our
> books into the same place, or into several same places.
> Even though we want to keep them, we might pile our
> books away in trunks, put them in the cellar or the attic,
> or in the bottoms of wardrobes, but we generally prefer
> them to be visible.

Even when hidden away, books are simply awaiting
their proper home in a fantasized library, where one day
they will converse with one another calmly.

My father's books were divided between my parents'
bedroom and a built-in, floor-to-ceiling bookcase
which I think my mother eventually convinced him
to install in the dining room. Her hope was, I suppose,
to rid the bedroom finally of the astonishing profusion
of volumes stacked in ragged piles about one side of
the room. She almost got her way. Even after most of
his books had been tucked away downstairs, my father
still contrived to have much of his collection tottering
by his bedside, from which position the whole edifice
would occasionally come tumbling down as he tried to
pluck a book from the middle of the pile. My mother
despaired, I think, less of the inexorable accumulation
(though she would sometimes scandalize my father with
the barbarous notion that he ought to 'get rid' of these
stray books) than of his unfathomable urge to keep a
good hundred or so perched perilously within reach at
all times.

This tower of books was a source of endless wonder
to me: an image of my father's incomparable knowledge.
But it was merely an intriguing adjunct to the greater part

of his library, which loomed over me in the shape of the bookcase whose upper, glass-guarded, shelves held the most precious and unattainable objects. I can still recall the precise placing of certain books: the slightly buckled slip-cover of a two-volume paperback edition of *War and Peace* took pride of place at the top left, the sturdy capital letter at the start of a parade of subordinate Russians, giving way, towards the other end of the shelf, to equally forbidding, if less weighty, Victoriana: Trollope, Eliot, the tattered green leather of a deluxe *Oliver Twist*, the only book I recall my father reading aloud to me (for years, I remembered little of it beyond the bumptious comic alliteration of the beadle). The rest of this upper stratum was punctuated by titles whose oddity fed my image of my father the reader. *The Confessions of an English Opium-Eater*, with its curious transparent dust jacket, was especially opaque to me, though somehow, I thought, related to Aldous Huxley's *Lotus Eaters* a few shelves below (I had no idea what was denoted by 'lotus' or 'opium' nor what the effects of ingestion might be). A little further down, the glass doors stopped above two open shelves on which stood a selection of Penguins: the bruised orangery of Lawrence, Waugh, Ford Madox Ford, Hemingway. These, while more accessible, held little interest. Only much later would I explore their interiors, and recognize there, in the last years of my father's life, the record of an aspect of him that was also a barely articulated point of contact between us.

In the summer of 1990, a couple of months after my father died, I finally found the courage to go through some boxes of his belongings which my brother Kevin had discovered tucked beneath the foot of his own bed. This cache of old documents seemed, to a mind not yet ready to tackle the more exacting task of examining the contents of my father's room, to exist at some consoling remove from my immediate memory of him. The first box I opened that afternoon had, I thought, an almost historical interest, rather than an emotional one. The box was packed with papers: some loose, others neatly inserted into plain brown card folders or held together in flimsy reams by archaic brass paperclips of the kind with a thick round top and two thin wings which splayed to keep the leaves in place. As I began to pull bunches of these papers from their hiding place, I realized that I had happened upon the archive of a period in my father's life about which I knew next to nothing. I knew this much: that in the mid-1960s he had graduated from University College Dublin with a degree in Economics and Politics, and that in the first year of his course he had also studied English and Philosophy, the same subjects in which I was about to begin my third year of study. In fact, I'd already inherited some tangible remains of my father's studies: from the bookcase downstairs, I had plucked numerous volumes for my own use, and been occasionally surprised to discover that my father's intellectual ambitions had once been rather more current, even radical, than his later literary tastes suggested. I remember how impressed I was to unearth at the back of a lower shelf a copy of Herbert Marcuse's *One-Dimensional Man*, and how I began (without ever discussing such things with my father) to piece together an image of him that was quite at odds with his taste for Trollope (whose works I deprecated without reading a single page) and his loftily dismissive reaction to my interest in the volumes of existentialist philosophy and Marxist political theory which he had left untouched for decades.

I have no doubt that my father felt some pride at my modest academic successes, but his reaction never got beyond the wry (and to me quite dismaying) suggestion that I might do well to restrict my reading to what he called 'the classics' before embarking on such esoteric studies. Only once did he ever comment directly on my own academic efforts. A few months before he died, I had been elated to have an essay returned (the topic, I think, was *The Tempest*) not only with an astonishingly high grade but with a tutor's comments which suggested that my father's warning at the start of my university career – to the effect that my hitherto dismal academic record might not augur well for a degree involving, as he put it, 'a lot of research' – could be challenged at last. He read my essay in silence. His curt response – only years later did it occur to me that its asperity hid a certain pleasure and surprise – was to note that my prose style was excessively 'Johnsonian'. I must have rehearsed that scene in my mind dozens of times since (such, in a way, is the orphan's tedious fate), as if stuck for ever in a moment of mute adolescent rage at having my ambitions reduced to a middle-aged quip. No doubt, of course, he was correct.

I assume, too, that he must at that moment have recalled his own time at the same university, the documentary evidence of which was spreading before me on the carpet a quarter of a century later. I had found, it turned out, my father's carefully filed notes from his days as a student. I can recall nothing of what was written on the hundreds of pages I pulled from the box that day. I don't think I spent much time reading their contents at all. Instead, I was transfixed by the image of my father that they brought to mind. I saw him, soberly suited and exhausted after a day's work (he must still, at that time, have held a minor position in what was then the Department of Post and Telegraphs), summoning the energy for an evening's lectures or solitary study. And I had a sense, suddenly, of the contingency of my own existence. Although I knew (and still know) only the barest details of his life at that time, I had to assume that my father's educational ambitions had as their goal his subsequent promotion in the civil service, and thus the possibility, not long after, of marriage. On his sedulous study, the remnants of which were piled around me, had depended the very possibility of my subsequent being.

At the bottom of the box, tucked to one side so that it had bent under the weight of the folders and loose papers above, was a small black notebook. The hard, shiny fabric of its spine had split, and crackled as I lifted and opened the book. The edges of the pages had obviously once been deep blue but had faded. I flicked quickly through the pages, from back to front: the notebook was empty but for a few leaves on which I recognized both my father's careful handwriting and the impress of his fountain pen. His hand, I noted, had put that instrument to a considerably defter use than I had so far managed, the thick nib here producing a surprisingly delicate script. Each of the ten or so pages on which my father's pristine blue letters were inscribed contained an outline of the life and works of a great Irish writer, from Jonathan Swift to James Joyce. On the last of these pages was a heading for Samuel Beckett, above an otherwise blank page. Why did Beckett deserve an entry but no comment? Perhaps my father simply had nothing to say about a writer whose works had conspicuously not made it, then or since, on to the shelves of his library. Or maybe (and the thought lifted my spirits) this was my father's devious little private joke at the expense of Beckett's love of silence and voids.

The notebook, with its broken spine, creaking cover and curious gilded legend – 'the Alwych Book with the all weather cover' – seemed an odd little memorial to my father's fastidious habits and dry sense of humour. It still pains me that, although I put it carefully aside that afternoon, I lost it somewhere in the intervening years. But it began to have a productive, faintly sentimental, afterlife when I discovered, a year later, that a single Dublin stationer still stocked these peculiar notebooks. I have since found a sort of comfort in the thought that all the identical books I have purchased since (I'm writing these words in one) amount, as they pile up on my desk at the rate of four or five a year, to a belated completion of my father's unfinished annotations. The Alwych notebook, it turns out, has been in production for the best part of the last century. Its current manufacturers, the Glasgow firm of John Reid, have proved sadly unclear, in response to my eccentric enquiries, about its exact provenance, but having recently uncovered an ancient receipt, are sure that it dates back at least to the mid-1920s. In its present incarnation, it seems miraculously unaltered. Its vaunted 'all weather cover' makes only the most cursory effort at a faux-leather appearance; one has the sense, instead, of handling something vaguely related to such mid-century materials as Bakelite, or the fragile heft of early vinyl records. The pale yellow pages, their dark blue edging fading pleasingly after only a few weeks' use, still tend to separate quickly from the glued spine, but are held in place, as forty years ago, by strong stitching. The whole thing rapidly takes on a scuffed, aged appearance, while remaining gratifyingly intact. It is the sort of object you imagine academics or scientists of half a century ago slipping out of their tweed pockets: a svelte amalgam of venerable tradition and quietly utilitarian design.

Despite its resonance as an object of pure nostalgia – a thing which, in the brief period I had it in my possession, was both the subject and the source of certain memories of my father – it seems also to suggest that a part of my father's life remained unfinished, unfulfilled. It will always be linked in my mind to a few scraps of paper discovered around the same time. I had long known that my father, as a young man, had had poetic ambitions. Indeed, as he occasionally reminded us, he had achieved some minor success: a poem of his had been published. Though I have no idea of the publication, I am sure that on at least one occasion he produced a tiny shred of newsprint as evidence. I recall nothing of the poem itself; if it ever really existed, it is now lost. I still possess, however, a small piece of paper, cut from a larger page, on which my father's name appears below some thirteen typewritten lines, entitled 'Newquay June 1969'; and I have the vaguest memory of my father recounting to me the tragedy that befell nine passengers of a boat which capsized in Galway Bay one summer.

On Sunday, 29 June 1969, the *Red Bank*, a 25-foot oyster boat, was taking parties of locals and holiday-makers out into the bay when, on its fifth trip, it overturned 200 yards from the pier head at Newquay. Newspaper reports published in the days following the accident are at first confused about the number of people lost, but they agree that most were children. In the end, they confirm that nine were drowned. The boat, it seems, was authorized to carry only a crew of three, but on this summer afternoon about forty passengers had been crammed on to its deck. One of the survivors, Sally Gaynor, aged thirteen, had seen her eight-year-old brother drown: 'The girls ran to one side of the boat and it overturned. I managed to swim from under it. I held on to a propellor and other people were holding on to me. I saw my brother Jimmy but there was nothing I could do and I knew he could not swim. I could not bear to watch him. I screamed and turned my head.'

Newquay June 1969

Do not grieve for them who died young
upon a Summer's eve;
Life's worth is not measured
by the span of days,
Nor hoary locks a fitting goal
for youth's ambitious gaze.
But in years to come;
When the lark sings high
over Corcamroe,
Give praise that in His wisdom
A far gentler hand than ours
Reached out and made a garland
of these nine fresh flowers.

Francis Dillon.

My father's poem is undated. I have no way of knowing when he composed his response to this terrible event. But reading it now, it seems less an adequate tribute to those drowned children than an excessively pious formulation of his own poetic persona. I cannot quite believe that the author of this fragment, whose first child had been born only seven weeks before the disaster, could in all seriousness begin a poem with the words 'Do not grieve for them who died young upon a Summer's eve'. Nor that he really means it when he concludes in his final lines that 'in His wisdom / A far gentler hand than ours / Reached out and made a garland of these nine fresh flowers'. It is not only the mawkishness of the metaphor that appals me; I simply cannot accept the content of that couplet, with its simplistic appeal to theological consolation. So allergic am I to the sentiment of the poem that I wonder now whether my father had already discerned in this, his first published verse (if this indeed is the one), a conventional stricture, a hampering strain of dogma, that put an end to his ambitions as a poet. Of all the objects of his that I have inherited, this is the one with which I would like to accost him still, to ask: what sort of man wrote these lines; what dream, later submerged in family life, work and illness, came clumsily to life here? What exactly was he thinking? And more: what did he feel as he put his name to this poem which, though it seems to me to display a sensibility which has quite missed the true horror of its occasion, must nonetheless have had for him some emotional significance, enough for him to have hidden the folded typescript away all those years? I wonder now whether this scrap of paper might not have been for my father the reminder of an unrealized dream, a memento from a life not lived. Or rather, of a career cut short by my own arrival that summer: a season which itself now exists only as a series of snapshots.

PHOTOGRAPHS

'Nothing tells memories from ordinary moments.
Only afterwards do they claim remembrance, on
account of their scars.'
— Chris Marker, *La Jetée*

'When will they invent a machine to know who I am?'
— Jacques Henri Lartigue

¶ Archive

In the winter of 1997, without, initially, giving much
thought to the significance of what I was doing, I began
spending my nights poring over a selection of photographs from the family hoard. For some months, I
had been huddled deep inside the folds of a depression
that had lately made it almost impossible for me to en-
gage by day with the postgraduate research I had left
Dublin to complete at a provincial university in the
south of England. In truth, I had made scarcely any
headway with my work since arriving two years earlier.
My ill-concealed lack of productivity was beginning
to tell against me in every respect: academic, financial
and personal. I felt myself constantly in flight from all
those who might notice some sign of the new vacuous-
ness of my being, the dull ache at the centre of my chest
that denoted my absconded hopes, plans and talents. As
deadlines passed and the promised doctoral thesis failed
to materialize time and again, I cast about desperately
for some prop to shore up my slowly spalling sense of
self, but succeeded only in adding to the confusion of a
mind long past hope of being cleared by its own efforts.
By this time, my second winter away from home, I had
made a comprehensively tangled mess out of all ties to
the world around me. During the summer of that year,
there were days when – having lain awake most of the
night, adrift between the vicious reality of my situation
and my increasingly fantastic notions of how best to end
my torment – I could hardly raise myself from my bed
before mid-afternoon. Once up, I was a frantic wreck
before the awful challenge of the day, quickly debilitated
again by the panic that overtook me when faced with the
simplest decision. Eventually, I was persuaded (it was
already autumn, and I realized that I had no memory

118

of the sun shining at all that summer) to drag myself, emaciated and, so I am told, actually grey in the face, to a doctor.

In the weeks that followed, my fogged brain began to respond slowly to the drugs I had immediately been prescribed. The deeper roots of my disarray would continue, for many months, to leach hope and energy from my life. But I was at least lucid enough to appreciate how far I had wandered from myself. And I had regained sufficient physical and mental function to begin to reflect on what had led me astray. Any doubts I might previously have had about the wisdom of a pharmacological cure for emotional torment were quickly dispersed: I could feel the disease as a palpably organic entity, a parasite. (Depression, wrote the glum Romanian philosopher E. M. Cioran, is as much physical as mental: left unchecked, it would attack even the fingernails.) The long-term effects of my breakdown – the word, I came to realize, should be understood in a literal, mechanical, sense – would take years to resolve. I do not think it was only as a result of a therapist's inevitable broaching of my family history, nor of the certainty that I had always had of my one day emulating my mother's plunge into depression, that I found myself mulling over the artifacts of my past. While I could not bring myself to face the demands of my unwritten thesis, I began an eccentric communion with the few photographs I had taken from our family home some years earlier. I entrusted something of myself, of my future, to them each night as I closed the door of a cramped bedroom and sat down at a tiny desk to peruse my archive once more. I realized that I had never really looked at them with anything other than a distant, even embarrassed, sense that the world they depicted was no longer a part of me. Now, however,

119

they seemed to have accosted me from the tattered box file where they had lain since my leaving the house. The process of their rediscovery had begun during the terrible summer just gone. One night, as I wrestled with my hopelessness and rage, I had suddenly, quite unaware of what I was doing, ripped a photograph of my parents from the wall of my bedroom and thrown myself on the bed, holding it tightly to my sobbing chest. I remember gradually realizing the absurdity of the gesture, and how I was utterly unable to communicate to the one person there (the lover whose life had contracted around my sapping and cruel presence) why my misery had taken such a melodramatic turn.

Each night, for perhaps an initial week or two, I would take the photographs out and place them one by one on the desk in front of me, until the whole collection had been divided among a few unruly piles. Each comprised photographs of a particular subject: myself, my parents individually or together, my family, various relatives, a few unknown persons. On those occasions, I would simply stare at the images in a sort of stupor, unsure what had motivated these long hours of desultory handling. Before long, however, another impulse took over: I began to write about the photographs. I had to overcome a distinct embarrassment. I told myself that the furtive marks I was about to make in the pages of a large softbound notebook were entirely unrelated to the halting words I spoke weekly to my therapist. Whatever I imagined I was doing with these photographs, it was not, I insisted, therapeutic. It was of another order entirely: some belated reckoning that might turn out to be unbearable, to undo all the therapist's good work (I could never decide if she was an angel or an idiot; but her unnerving silences seemed to have freed something in me, even if I didn't yet believe in it). I resolved to describe what I saw in these photographs, rather than indulge in any excessive reminiscence or conjecture about their significance. What I wanted, I think, was at last to recall simply what I saw there, no longer to feel so detached from the scant remains of my own past. I had long been fascinated by – and now re-read obsessively – the pages of *Camera Lucida*, Roland Barthes's melancholy reflection on photography and death, which treat of certain photographs of his mother uncovered after her death. I had already half mythologized my own collection according to the details of Barthes's troubled engagement with the image of his mother. He writes: 'according to these photographs, sometimes I recognized a region of her face, a certain relation of nose and forehead, the movement of her arms, her hands. I never recognized her except in fragments, which is to say that I missed her *being*, and that therefore I missed her altogether.' Now, I thought, I would test my own photographs against the misery that kept me confined to my room. Perhaps I would recognize something there; and if I didn't, I would at least discover the consolation of expressing my failure.

I began nightly to write a few lines (in my exhausted state, I could manage no more) about a particular photograph. Over a period of some weeks, I completed eleven fragments: each one numbered and appended with a brief statement of (so far as I could discern) when, where and by whom the snapshot was taken. I recall now that it was only, each time, by a prolonged act of concentration that I could begin to piece together precisely what I was looking at. Certainly, the bare essentials of each scene were usually clear to me: it was the details that seemed completely foreign. I sometimes spent hours simply sitting and staring, before certain spaces, objects or textures became recognizable, and I started to fit them to the abstract image I had in my head of each occasion or era made visible there.

The first photograph that I tried to describe was taken when I was about seven: it shows my brothers and me sitting rather nervously in a row in the gym of our primary school. At the end of a day's photographing of individual pupils, we had been brought specially from our respective classes to sit for this picture of what might well have been the only trio of brothers in the school at that time. There is, really, nothing else of note about the photograph, and in my short written account of it I have remarked only that I recall being even more uncomfortable in front of the camera than I look. Here I am again, according to the second passage in the notebook, perched on a deckchair in the back garden: an insignificant image but for the barely visible fraying of the fabric of the chair around its metal frame. Years later, somebody (it may well have been me) would fall straight through the torn seat. And again: proudly straddling a brand-new bicycle, aged seven; or a small blur on a rug five years earlier; or squinting towards my father at the height of a summer's holiday in Kerry; or glumly edging from the frame, aged thirteen, on the occasion of my brother's confirmation.

Those paragraphs comprise only my first broaching of a territory from which I retreated before long. Which is not to say that the other photographs – of the world my parents inhabited before my birth – did not intrigue me: I gazed at them for hours, became obsessed with certain scenes depicted there, but they never made it into my written record of the collection. I seem to have avoided looking at photographs of my parents without me, as if I was not yet willing to accept that the collection as a whole was the evidence of their disappearance. Why was I unable to write about the photographs of my parents in the same way? I am quite prepared to believe that my depression was a function of an incomplete process of mourning (if the truth be told, a process not even begun: mourning, surely, requires some voicing of one's grief, and this was exactly what I could not begin to attempt). But if so, my solitary scribblings didn't get me much further along the route to a complete reckoning with my loss; instead, I became entranced by the details and the surfaces of these other images. I may not have been able to write about them, but it was these photographs of a world in which I was not yet present that appeared then (and seem now) to contain the most telling memories of all.

I have the photographs in front of me now. There are thirty-six of them: the first taken some time in the mid-1930s, the last in the summer of 1985. About a third of them – the fraction that I described in the notebook which I have also just unearthed – belong to my lifetime. I am present in almost all of these. The others, mostly black and white, show my parents: first individually, then, briefly, together, before I join them in various sunlit gardens and parks. I remember that as I looked at these photographs in that depressed autumn, I felt as though I were seeing some of them for the first time. Having recently faded so far from the world around me that I thought myself unrecognizable, I seemed to discover in them a means to verify my own existence. Here, at least, I thought, I have been really present. I imagined that if I could reconstruct those fleeting moments of proven being before the camera, I might be able to work out why I had now apparently evanesced to the point where, on being photographed, I barely credited that I would register on film. This was not an entirely fanciful notion: snapshots from this time show me as an emaciated wraith, and I recall very clearly my feeling that each time there was a little less of me to photograph.

¶ *Reliquary*

I had never seen most of these photographs of my parents until they were both dead. What I was looking at as I stared at them alone in my room was a world that, for me, had only come into existence with the disappearance of the figures at its centre. At least, this is how I remember it: that the images of them I found in their room after my father's death allowed me to picture for the first time what they looked like and the world they inhabited. Can this be true? Did they really never present me with the evidence of their lives prior to my own? Was there never an evening when, together, we passed around the mostly black and white images, my father ruefully noting his full head of hair, my mother recalling school-friends and flatmates? It seems an eccentric lapse: to behave as if our family had no visual history worth sharing. Not for the first time, I compared my own photographic inheritance unfavourably with the means I imagined other families employing to protect theirs: the photograph album's material repository and the ritual (by which one comes to know the photograph as well as, if not better than, the moment captured there) of communal perusal.

The family photograph has not always been subject to the same curatorial regime. In the earliest days of the medium, the daguerreotype – a print whose solid metallic base held an image of such fragility that it only manifested itself at a specific attitude to the light, and might be erased if exposed too long – was kept in its own individual case. Many of these cases have, of course, survived: their varnished wooden exteriors and rich velvet insides attest to the reverence with which the faint image would once have been treated. The clearest evidence of their special status is to be glimpsed in

125

mid-nineteenth-century photographs themselves, where whole families can sometimes be seen gathered around a daguerreotype of an absent or deceased relative. Often, the photographed picture is actually invisible. Still hidden in its miniature cabinet, it nevertheless accrues to itself a care and veneration which seems to be based as much on touch as on vision. Semi-orphaned siblings surround their remaining parent, who holds the tiny sliver of a lost spouse's memory: the whole family reaches out to touch the frail relic. Mothers whose children have died in infancy cradle minute reminders of exhausted little bodies. Seeing the photograph is only one way of making it mean something: its presence is as resonant (perhaps even more so, if the image has started to fade) as its appearance.

For the Victorians, such reminders of the photograph's tactility extended its significance, and, by means of an impressive variety of ancillary objects and appended matter, ensured that the physical spell of the picture spread around it like the shrine that threatens to overwhelm the relic of a saint. All manner of things were attached to the photograph. (We ought not to conclude that the picture simply needed its mnemonic power upgraded: image and object formed a circuit of reciprocal energies.) The scrap of hair, secreted in a locket alongside the photograph, is only the most obvious addition: this traditional memento might be further worked to form a decorative border to the photograph, or even woven to compose a consoling verse. A thriving domestic industry, overseen mostly by the women of a family, affixed poems, flowers both dried and artificial, fragments of clothing, certificates of birth or death, elaborately executed drawings or paintings in which the photographed figure might appear to perform in a pious or nostalgic tableau. In turn, the photograph could itself become an adjunct to a more solid piece of domestic furniture: sewn on to a cushion or inserted into a shrine to a deceased child. By such means, the humble image was made to live again according to the new chronology of remembrance, of which our modest photographic albums seem only to have understood the barest outlines. Still, they preserve an element of order and ritual which is quite foreign to my own experience of the photographs I own.

¶ *Lumber room*

The photographs I have managed to salvage from the house of my childhood – that is, those of them that I have not, over the years, lost, foolishly discarded or (even worse) given away – are subject to no visible principle of organization whatsoever. Protected but uncelebrated, they have sat (apart from that brief period when they became a nightly obsession) in a succession of more or less forgotten corners. Occasionally, I have taken one or two out and displayed them for a while. Looking back, I realize that I have only ever chosen those which seemed to have some vague artistic merit: the particularly striking composition of a photograph of my father on a Parisian street half a century ago (reminiscent of the work of Robert Doisneau, though more affecting because less sure of its own appeal to the romance of the city), or the fancied resemblance of a picture of my mother's family in the 1930s to something seized on by August Sander: a study, say, in the taxonomy of rural respectability. Or I might simply have been drawn by an image that seemed to accord with an almost caricatured notion of what a 'family photograph' ought to look like: awkward and poetic, luminously ordinary. I invested some energy in these decisions, but risked no reflection that could be said to have properly reckoned with their real meaning for me. Then, for that short, and wretched, period in my late twenties, certain photographs of my parents became, as I lingered over them, allegorical images of my own sorry state of mind. Still, I could do little more than stare stupidly at them in turn, summoning no sense of connection (or even of debilitating distance) that might turn itself into a narrative or a nexus of emotion or memory. In short: still no meaning. (I thought that 'meaning' was what I was after.)

It has never occurred to me to find them a more satisfactory home than the tattered box file where they currently reside. My reluctance to dignify them with the sense of a collection by putting them in an album stems, I suppose, from my furtive, shameful relationship with them: from some sense that I'd have both to face up to them and let them go if I gave them a more permanent arrangement. I marvel at those who can pull out a volume of family snapshots and see there a continuity that I find unfathomable. How can one look at these things and not feel that they are spinning in some chaotic parallel universe into which one might be sucked at any moment? What unimaginable reckoning has taken place that allows a person to act as if at home with the archive of lost time? In the face of my own small gathering, I either want to flee as far from them as possible, or am rooted to the spot for hours. And if I have recently, at last, found a middle ground between those two impulses, it may be only because I have forced myself (and here is the evidence) to attempt a minimal description of what these images of my parents look like. For that is, I suspect, what I had never really considered: these photographs' status as mere records, of something, of somebody, that I have done my best to disguise by a blithe or morose gaze which never properly saw them in the first place.

The photographs in my collection have been in my sole possession for almost a decade and a half. For some reason, I cannot look at them without noting this fact, which means that soon I will have had them for as long as my parents were married. The calculation is meaningless, but reminds me that I think of them as engaged together on a round-about journey. For the most verifiably ancient – a pair of photographs that show, separately, my mother and father, and that were probably taken within a year or two of each other – the time spent as part of my collection will have been only a brief interlude in their history. Before that, they may well have been hidden away in albums belonging to my parents' respective families, oblivious to the secret affinity that would one day bring them together. They might have been displayed, on top of a pair of brooding, crudely veneered cabinets, in rooms reserved for especially respectable visitors and sober or celebratory occasions. I imagine them looking down, these two pictures (whose faces we will meet before long), on christening parties and funerals, visiting priests and departing emigrants. Or perhaps (because in their different ways they record moments that are intimate as well as public) they will have been tucked at parental bedsides or hung in more frequented living rooms. They may not have been treated with the respect due a photograph taken by a professional at all, but considered as mementoes to be regularly regarded: reminders, in fact, of love.

Later photographs inherited from my parents divide more readily into those that might once have graced a sideboard or been hung on a parlour wall and those (too banal, too informal, or simply too obviously part of an explosion in the sheer quantity of photographs taken) that probably emerged only rarely from an envelope, an album, or a shoebox. Looking at them now, I wonder how my parents chose to bring these photographs and not others with them when they set up home together. Of course, they may have been taken from their respective homes later (maybe much later: photographs, after all, change hands most often when somebody dies). Even established in their new home (my home), they would never have been seen like this, together. They would have stayed in the separate drawers of my parents' dressing table, in different boxes and suitcases shoved under the middle of their bed, in crumbling brown envelopes at the back of the wardrobe. They ended up, in other words, in all the places where my brothers and I later found them.

My parents could not be said to have been keen photographers. They photographed only our annual family holidays and, at other times of the year, the most important occasions: First Communions, confirmations, the visits of emigrant family members. But even as I write this, my certainty slips away again. There are enough photographs of me extant to suggest that the camera came out, sometimes, for a spontaneous snapshot or two. And I recall also a few stray images of myself that are now definitively lost: standing in the front garden, dressed in a Scout's uniform and dreading (justifiably, as it turned out) the boisterous, pointless rigours of an annual camping trip; the whole family gathered beneath the blossoms of my grandfather's apple trees; a selection of holiday snaps in which I squint against the sun and try my best to imagine myself elsewhere.

Perhaps my sense of the paucity of photographs in our household derives instead from the fact that, once developed and deposited, still in their envelopes, in my parents' bedroom, they were so rarely brought out. Or maybe it comes from the perennially disappointing appearance of the images themselves. My parents seem always to have chosen the most unattractive sort of print: the texture of so many of these images is weirdly striated, knurled, thickened by a patina that can sometimes obscure all detail. I remember my surprise, on examining the occasional snapshot given to us by relatives, that a photograph could be so much clearer and more luminous. You would think, sifting through a decade and a half of our photographed history, that a thick membrane had grown between ourselves and the world: everything is slightly out of focus, trapped behind a veil that persists till the very last photograph of my parents together, taken just weeks before my mother died. In the end, though, the odd obscurity of our family photographs has nothing to do with the quality of the actual prints, but is traceable to this clear and wrenching memory: that long before this final snapshot appeared, we had stopped taking pictures.

In the winter I spent emerging from the worst of my depression, as I sat and looked at these photographs from my childhood, I was struck by how much more lucid were the monochrome photos of my parents dating from before my birth. They were not only sharper, but more various, more relaxed, more obviously celebratory. Our family photographs, by contrast, invariably capture static poses: they show us behaving as if the presence of the camera were a command rather than an invitation. In the throes of my depression, I was unsurprised to find that we rarely managed to smile (though I suspect, with a less fogged eye, that our solemn expressions were usually the result of a mistimed exposure rather than collective misery). I realized that I knew very little of my parents' lives before my birth, and next to nothing about the years immediately prior to their marriage in 1968. The photographs were unlikely to fill the gaps in my knowledge, but I was sure that if I concentrated hard enough on them, something would come to light. The later images in which I appeared, after all, had yielded, after long gazing beneath the weak ellipse of light above my desk, numerous tiny forgotten details of my childhood. Glimpsed through a window: a white plastic flowerpot which sat there, its contents long dead, until the day I left the house. Seen flourishing above my infant head in our garden: a lilac tree that had stopped flowering by the time I quit the garden for the last time. I became similarly obsessed with the specifics of the earlier photographs. In my doleful state, I thought I might find in the photographs of my parents some means of reconstituting what I remembered of them, and what I had never known.

¶ *Fragment*

Photographs of my mother make up only a small fraction of the collection before me, but the full span of her life is represented, with only two notable breaks in the continuum. The first corresponds, I think, with my mother's leaving home and moving to Dublin. Suddenly, it seems, it's the sixties, and she has cut and styled her hair into a soft bouffant which is still there, somewhat stiffened, in the last photograph for which she sat. (This final picture also marks the end of the second gap in my mother's photographic history.) The first breach is notable too for an abrupt switch from black and white to colour. She becomes, in the muted decor of several sixties interiors – her sixties are not the garish years of nostalgic cliché, just as my photographed seventies are not yet the lurid decade of kitsch remembrance – recognizably the person I recall, posing (always a touch more elegant than those around her) with friends and flatmates in comfortably dull sitting rooms.

But first: here is a tiny image obviously torn from an album. A map-like portion of black paper has come away with the photograph. Where the decoratively serrated edge has been torn, and the picture begun to lift from its backing, it is clear that the print itself is extremely fragile, much thinner than those which come before or after it. This picture also stands out as the only photograph in the whole collection to be tinted, very slightly, with a faint sepia tone. I have always assumed that it was taken by a professional: it is one of several showing my mother and her siblings, each image posed in almost the same arrangement (my mother and her two brothers standing or sitting in a line, the younger girls coaxed in front of them one by one over the course of a decade or so). The photographer has been rather careless with his lighting:

the photograph is over-exposed, and the four children pictured here (the two youngest of my mother's sisters, I assume, are not yet born) as they sit beneath a pale, blurred hedge are squinting as they smile towards the camera. My mother is not quite 'herself' yet; she grimaces, barely recognizable, out of the centre of the shot, flanked by two mischievous-looking brothers and her toddler sister. The date, I calculate, is about 1940.

Almost all of these pictures of my mother – from the black and white forties to the colour sixties – make perfect sense to me. Their dates may be vague, but their locations are easily read. Even when, as later in the photographs of my mother in Dublin, a series of unknown faces starts to intrude, I still have the sense that I know who or what I'm looking at: a discernible family history unfolds here. Certain details recall what I know. My mother's father kept greyhounds; here is one of them, straining at a leash held tightly by my young uncle. The youngest of my aunts has been very ill: here she is looking slight for her age at the front of the sibling group; my mother tugs her pigtails and laughs.

My mother moves recognizably across these photographs, slowly becoming the image of her that I remember. The photographs of my father, by contrast, are often unfathomable. There is little sense of a family here at all: no record of his parents or two sisters, no evidence of a life together. Only a single, formal, photograph of my father hints at a family group, waiting, just beyond the frame, for him to compose himself for a studio photographer. He seems to have been thrust into the world without ritual or celebration, without regular photographic gatherings of the sort which ensure that the photographs of my mother are so easily legible. Here he is, a teenaged blur, apparently quickening his pace to escape the viewfinder of a photographer on a Dublin street (its width, behind him, suggests that it might be O'Connell Street). Though the image is hazy and has faded badly, his fixed stare, straight ahead, is still recognizable. Beside him, less distinct, is another young man, who hangs back slightly behind his friend, but looks directly at the camera.

Behind them, two girls, arm in arm, also address the camera openly; their coats are tightly buttoned, their heads covered with scarves. Are they together, these four? It is impossible to say – the two young women certainly seem to think that they're part of the photographer's composition. Only my father looks uncomfortable, even irritated, at being photographed. He seems to have deliberately ignored the photographer who has just stepped into the middle of the pavement, and who will presumably, in a moment, offer a snapshot of this hurrying foursome. If the photographer has any sense, he will ignore the rather haughty youth at the centre of his frame and concentrate his efforts on his slouching companion and the eager duo behind. But it seems he may have succeeded in persuading my father to part with his name, address and cash. The fleeting moment on the street has ended up as an image of my father that I cannot parse: it tells me nothing and connects to no image I already possess of him.

Nor can I identify the three women and one man who flank my father in the sunshine one day in 1946 (this is one of the few photos in my collection with an inscribed date). My father is quite handsome, almost pretty, though less at ease than his anonymous friends. I can relate almost nothing of his life at this point. I know that he left school four years earlier to work as a messenger boy for the post office. I know that in the intervening years of the 'Emergency' he trained as a member of the civil defence force, and stopped one morning on his way to work to watch two fighter planes, considerably adrift from their planned courses, chasing each other in the sky above the city. I have an idea, derived from some admonishing lecture delivered when I was a child not much given to 'making my own entertainment', that his life was an endless round of tennis and card games. And although this photograph tells me that he might have had more on his mind, I can't help suspecting that one of these five will find herself, any minute now, on the sidelines as the other four take up their rackets.

The most intriguing set of images among the photos of my father is the half dozen or so taken some time in the late 1940s or early 1950s on a journey round France. I had known for years, before discovering these, that he and a friend (the only friend I ever knew my father to have had: he turned up at our house once, after my mother died, and he himself died a week before my father) had spent some time there. I recall my father telling me that everywhere he went, he still saw evidence of the war, and that at some point in the journey he had, alarmingly, driven a car (my father never learned to drive, though I also recall – and may have imagined – another story that has him driving from Dublin to Cork, quite illegally, on some official civil service business).

Clearly, my father's friend (known only as Slevin) had an eye for a picture. He photographed his travelling companion looking extraordinarily dashing against a selection of exotic backdrops. There he is in shirtsleeves on a street somewhere in the south, cigarette dangling from his fingers, framed by palm trees, the windows of the building behind him shuttered against the heat. He exhibits, to my surprise, a repertoire of matinée-idol poses that I'd never have guessed he could deploy. So iconic does he look – brooding against the balustrade of what I take to be a Parisian bridge, looming as a stark silhouette in the doorway of a Crédit Lyonnais, square-jawed and just out of focus as his boat pulls into, or away from, a nameless harbour – that, forty years later, a friend and I would attempt, ineptly, to replicate the faded elegance of those photographs. But no matter how louchely I tried to light a Gauloise while slouching by the entrance to a Métro station, I could never capture the unaccountable presence which my father exhibits here. Neither, it seems, could he. In subsequent snapshots, he appears already middle-aged; his former reticence before the camera has got the better of him again. Photographed at a ballroom table ten years later (a glittering stave of musical notation plays on the wall above his head), his efforts to look casual haven't quite come off. Lounging back in his chair, he succeeds only in separating himself from the rest of the group.

¶ *The stock*

A family photograph is supposed to recall us to a presence with which we are already familiar. But its effect is often to make a well-known physiognomy appear suddenly alien. At certain junctures in *À la recherche du temps perdu*, Proust reminds us that the photograph can as effectively distance us from the remembered face as recall it for us. When the narrator's grandmother is about to die, she becomes, he tells us, like a photograph of herself:

> the process that automatically occurred in my eyes when I caught sight of my grandmother was indeed a photograph. We never see the people who are dear to us save in the animated system, the perpetual motion of our incessant love for them, which, before allowing the images that their faces present to reach us, seizes them in its vortex and flings them back upon the idea that we have always had of them, makes then adhere to it, coincide with it.

Photography, and the proximity of death, tear the face from its home and memory and set it adrift in time, where we find that we have failed to recognize the faces we know best.

Here is my mother, sitting on her mother's knee; beside them are her father and elder brother. The photograph finds the young family in front of a whitewashed wall. To the right of the group – a peculiar insertion into the frame, this – is a sash window, one pane of which has been broken, adding a jagged rectangle of black to the pale background. It is also a clue to the precise spot where the family has been invited to pose. I surmise that the window belongs to a former farmhouse that had now been given over to livestock: to the photographer's right is the new house, which was itself superseded: my grandparents left it for a bungalow a few miles away. In the photograph, they are seated; only one leg of each chair is visible, so that they almost appear to float unsupported before the pallid, stained backdrop. The image has clearly been produced by a professional (it is, in fact, a postcard). The chairs have been brought out into the sun; everybody squints slightly. If I've guessed the location correctly, it is morning (the old house faced east, the new one south). The family is dressed for the occasion and posed with just the proper combination of formality and ease. The father's dark three-piece suit dominates the whole field of the photograph; his son grimaces and holds one chubby hand to his face. The mother is less distinct. Her hair has been caught by the breeze and she is further blurred by a fading (or overexposed) area to the left of the frame that renders her faintly spectral beside her husband. Her coat is shapeless, and her polka-dot dress almost indistinguishable from that of her daughter, who sits on her lap, mirroring her brother's sullen gesture.

About my grandmother, I remember almost nothing. There are only two images of her that I can bring into focus. The first sees me playing on the gravel outside her house. A sandpit had been filled by the door: a photograph shows me, aged about four, standing proprietorially in front of it, clutching a bucket and a large stick that has taken over from a tiny spade which lies on the ground beside me. I had expanded the scope of my excavations and begun to dig on the path down to the road. What I remember is simply my grandmother telling me to stop, and directing me back to the sand. After she died (I was five), I'd recall this moment with a terrible, secret shame each summer. The other tiny fragment of her that I recall has me sitting in her living room: my grandmother is offering to fill the egg-cup in front of me with whiskey.

This photograph of my mother's family has always seemed to me to be confusingly doubled. On the one hand, it might almost be a study in a certain sociological moment: 'Ireland in the 1930s'; or, more generally, 'prewar farm life' (in which case its national character would disappear: this could be anywhere, any time in the first fifty years of the twentieth century). A good deal of what I read here is merely cultural: it has strictly nothing to do with what I remember of these individuals, and rather too much to say about their circumstances, about the obvious care with which they have prepared for this unusual morning when (perhaps for the first time since my mother was born) the family was to be photographed. It might equally be an illustration of how such people comported themselves before a visiting photographer in the days before it was usual for a family like this to own a camera.

The photograph is both a historical artifact and a

reminder of something I've never actually known. My grandparents appear here like those images of past fashions of which Baudelaire wrote that 'the living substance gave suppleness to what appears too stiff to us'. These figures inhabit their clothes, and the space around them, with a strange intimacy. All the markers of chronological distance are at the same time those of lived, tactile experience. It is this which gives such a photograph its specific power to thrust me into a temporal conundrum: what appears here as the very texture of the subjects' lives is also what leaves me staring at them from a debilitating distance. And yet, I can transcend those details and grasp nothing less than the essence of my memory of my grandparents. The photograph rehearses with uncanny accuracy the clarity of the images of them I recall. My grandfather's suit is almost unchanged – but for the upward sweep of a lapel and his double-breasted waistcoat – from the suit I remember him as always wearing. His huge mottled hands and shock of white hair (here subdued for the occasion) hover, in my memory, just above their photographic doubles. My grandmother requires a greater degree of concentration, but still she seems as if she might step into either of the two moments I remember her as inhabiting.

In short, the photograph is like one of those images that appear in biographies, accompanying the narrative of the subject's prehistory but never quite matching up with it. And at the centre of this particular photograph sits a fascinating blank: a hole in the surface of the image to which I am able to give a name but which I cannot look at without feeling myself alienated from the whole picture. It is the figure of my mother, whose face is quite unlike that of the being I knew. Everything in this frame is in some (even if tentative) way readable and recuperable in terms of my own experience, except, appallingly, my mother. So unfamiliar is this infant that I have sometimes been convinced that it cannot be her. I have tried to imagine a circumstance in which she would not appear, in which the unknown face that looks at me is in fact that of one of her sisters (the boy, by contrast, is totally familiar: my uncle's expression is unmistakably that of several generations of the family). But brute chronology is against me: as the second child and first daughter, it can only be my mother who gazes out of this photograph with a look that undoes all my efforts at recollection, at making this image coincide with the facts I know.

When I first discovered it (after both my parents were dead), this photograph of my mother came as something of a shock. While I was able to find in it so many reminders of a specific history – a history that was both mine and something more abstract, more 'historical' – my mother seemed to be entirely absent. She was reduced to a photographic archetype: the infant dandled on her mother's knee. I could find nothing of her there, and therefore nothing of myself. And this absence, this feeling that she was manifestly present but just out of reach, was distinctly painful.

I put aside this first instance of my own photographic history and began to concentrate on an image of
my father. He is aged about seven: the occasion is his
First Communion, and he is photographed in a studio,
looking so like me over forty years later that, having
misplaced my own Communion photos, I can still picture them hovering just below the surface of this one,
identical in almost every detail. I found this photograph
not long after my father died, and although I'd been reminded all my life of my resemblance to him, I was still
shocked to discover the extent of the similarity between
our seven-year-old selves. In fact, I half suspected that
I'd been dressed, in the early summer of 1976, precisely
to replicate this photograph. Certainly, no other child I
knew had suffered the bizarre indignity of a tailor-made,
short-trousered, three-piece suit, and as I looked at my
father's costume – only a handkerchief and the barely
visible clip of a pen in his top pocket distinguished his
get-up from my own – I felt as if he'd perpetrated a bitter
practical joke across the decades.

On the reverse of the print, a date has been stamped
in purple ink – '23 May' – but the year is illegible. My
dating of this image is thus imprecise, though I have always imagined that the year is 1935. But as my father was
born in November of 1928, this would place the photograph – assuming that he was seven years old at the time
of his First Communion – somewhere in 1936. And so,
by this simple belated recalculation, my father's image
begins to edge a little closer to the earliest photograph
of my mother. The studio photograph, pictured, as the
reverse of the image informs me, 'by the Owl Studio'
(the first and last letters of the studio's name are the eyes
of a pair of birds in profile: eyes almost as wide as those

of my father on the other side). A vaguely defined back-drop hovers behind the young boy: an odd combination of two looming trompe-l'œil trees or bushes and a black-and-white-squared tiled floor receding into the distance. The scene abuts awkwardly and unconvincingly an intricately patterned carpet on which stands a small table with a glass vase full of flowers. My father's hand grips the leading corner of the table, his arm held stiffly in his suit; from his short trousers his legs descend in pale socks and highly polished shoes. The white rosette in his lapel is overexposed and glares out from his dark jacket like a puff of white ectoplasm in a spiritualist photograph of half a century earlier. He holds his head awkwardly above a collar which looks stiff and too new. His hair has been plastered to one side (which recalls my father's insistence on painfully scraping my hair into the same style for my Communion photo). Palely glaring towards the photographer with a look that is half terror, half curiosity, he is a little startled light bulb of nervous energy above the gloomy stricture of his garb.

The image is a mass of antique detail. It fixes its subject rigorously within the constraints of the past. The scene is so rigid in its arrangement that there appears at first to be little of my father there at all. It seems an image stalled at the level of the formal pose, and therefore susceptible to no imaginative investment beyond the rigours of a certain sort of knowledge. And that knowledge is scant. I can connect this diminutive figure only with a scattering of clichés: the formal occasion of a studio portrait, the demands of the photographer (hinted at by the rigidity of the gesture that connects my father to the edge of the table) and of the parents who hover outside the frame. I picture a familiar strictness in his father's demeanour, but cannot see my grandmother at all. The only biographical fact to which I can attach the photograph at first comes from my knowing that not long after it was taken, my father would awake one morning to find himself paralysed from the waist down. He will spend months immobilized, before whatever undiagnosed catastrophe has befallen him will finally lift and he will be able to walk again. In the meantime, he will have been trundled about the streets in a wheelbarrow (or so the rather picturesque story he told had it).

All of this seems to situate my father in a distant, almost legendary past. It is as if photography itself were to blame for his paralysis, as if he has been scrubbed, starched and pressed flat by the weight of formality. And yet this is also the photographic instant at which I have imagined that my father comes alive in my memory. In the long course of my struggle to connect the images with myself, I became neurotically convinced of their fragility. I decided to photocopy those I thought most significant. The copies would ensure that the iconic originals remained untarnished by my melancholically regular handling. This photograph of my father proved, however, impossible to copy accurately. Beneath the photocopier's light, the image almost vanished. The studio sank into nothingness; my father's suit became an oblong void, only slightly more black than the surrounding gloom. Out of the darkness, a few details glinted like bright satellites orbiting the dead world of my father's presence at the centre. A few specks of pure white still insisted: the edges of the flowers, a single sock, the pallid insignia of the handkerchief, the rosette and a pristine collar. His hand still clung, as if severed, to the now obscured edge of the table. For all its newly darkened strangeness, this was the moment when I could say for the first time that the face which hovered above these few details was recognizably that of my father. What had appeared in the actual photograph to be the unknowable face of a young boy gazing at the camera six decades earlier became, in the photocopy, an expression I knew, half-quizzical, half-proud.

¶ *The unique being*

In my father's Communion photograph there is a fragility about him that is quite absent from the other photographs of him I possess. There, he controls his own image successfully; here, he has not quite managed to appear wholly confident, or pious, or pleased with himself. It is a face with which I felt I could identify. The photograph's resemblance to those of my own First Communion was only the most obvious connection: really, I identified with my father's inability here to become properly part of the surrounding formal scenography. I was convinced that this quality in the image could not be explained by his age. It was not only that my father was a child here, but that he revealed, inadvertently, a tenderness that I felt I recognized and at the same time could not conjure out of my own repertoire of memory-images. Such, at least, was my imagined connection with the image as I set it aside and turned to another.

In a photograph of my mother aged, it seemed, about eighteen, another sort of exception presented itself: here, my mother looked more assured, more at ease, than I had ever seen her. A group of seven young women stands in bright sunlight in front of a sturdy greenhouse. The occasion is not difficult to ascertain: one of them holds a book, and two others clutch rolls of paper; they have just, I am certain, received their Leaving Certificates. The scene is the exterior of a school in north Kerry half a century ago. They are wearing, on this perfect summer day, a variety of dresses which place them earlier, as if they are modestly sporting the fashions of the previous decade. But they do not look dated; they have dressed up for the occasion and they all face the camera proudly, squinting slightly into the sunlight. Most

of them look slightly awkward. They seem, in the way
that the youth of the past often do, to be much older than
their late teens; a few already look almost maternal. My
mother stands at the back, the tallest of the group, her
body turned slightly at an angle so that I notice first the
elegance of her jacket and the way she faces the photographer with a poise which her classmates, for all their
eager address to the camera, seem to lack.

I am touched by the notion that my mother is not like
the others: that this photograph shows me a singularity which is in fact detachable from the scenography of
milieu (provincial), of education (predictably religious:
a photograph taken on the same day from a slightly different angle shows the group surrounding a beaming
nun) or of history. This idea seems to come from a particular attitude towards the camera, as much as from
the simple observation (a fact I remark upon with some
pride) that my mother is darkly glamorous compared
to her sun-blinded companions. She has, I tell myself,

a particular aura about her in which doubtless one can already see the modest ambition that will take her away from this place within a few years, a move without which my own existence would be impossible.

¶ *The bridge*

There is a single photograph that connects my mother's move to the city with my own existence: the first I possess of my parents together. It was the only photograph of my parents that I had ever displayed where others could see it; for several years I had pinned it to the walls of a succession of bedrooms. It was a tiny reminder, I imagined, of their continued presence in my life, but also allowed me to see my parents as somehow detached from my recollection of them, cast in the roles of young lovers from another age. Later, a larger, framed version hovered on the wall above my bed, just out of my field of vision, as I slid the original from the pile in front of me. I realized that I had in fact never properly considered the content or significance of this photograph. It had functioned as a compensatory talisman, as a way of not addressing the collection as a whole, but of extracting from it a fetishized and venerated memento, in the process defusing its true mnemonic charge. As I held its edges now, careful not to mark its fragile sheen, it began, slowly, to undo the whole skein of recollection I had woven around the earliest images of my parents.

It is one of only two photographs I own of my parents together, unaccompanied by family or friends. The photograph was taken on O'Connell Bridge in Dublin. It shows my parents crossing the bridge at night. It is not difficult to work out that they are heading north: behind them are the faint outlines of two telephone boxes I remember clearly. Above them, out of the darkness, a neon sign announces 'Shannon Travel Ltd, Westmoreland St'. The same faces have already looked at me from other photographs, pictures I had buried in a kind of prehistory and regarded as if part of a photographic archaeology. These earlier scenes had yielded

151

up their significance – the glimpse of a gaze with which I could connect – precisely, I now realized, because of their distance. The uniqueness of those faces had been surrounded by so much abstractedly archaic detail. It was the contrast between their expressions and what surrounded them that had allowed me to acknowledge my parents.

This nocturnal scene presented a different genre of photographic drama. My initial confusion was a matter of pure chronology: they looked so young. I had always thought that my parents must have met sometime in the early 1960s. They had married in 1968. But I could not connect that knowledge with what I saw here. There seemed such a vast distance between the couple in the picture and the earliest photographs of their married life, of which, in the chronological advance of the collection, I would soon become a part. Maybe, I reasoned, my unease arose from a simple absence in my own knowledge of those years. I had (and still have) no idea when my parents met.

What I encountered here was – in an odd way, for the very first time – the image of my parents as a couple. The darkness which separates them starts as a gap in the balustrade of the bridge and extends downwards through the centre of the image. It keeps them apart but it is not empty. My father's arm extends behind my mother's back. Does his hand touch her lightly as they cross the bridge in front of the photographer who will shortly offer this image of an intimacy which only he has noticed? It is a warm night; my father has taken off his coat and carries it loosely over his arm. A breeze has caught my mother's skirt so that it moves ahead of her out of the frame towards the brightness of O'Connell Street, towards which her smile advances too.

The photograph intrigues and appals me for this reason: it may be that I would never have existed but for this night, but, perhaps, for this very moment. Could it be that my parents do not yet know each other well? Is this not only the first photographic evidence I have of their relationship but – and the thought sends me back to the image, plunged now in a sort of vertigo, stranded on the bridge between actuality and a past without me – the very first photograph of them together? If so, it may be that the moment they were accosted by the photographer (I imagine my father gallantly, awkwardly amused, giving his name and address) was the very moment they began to consider themselves a couple. In the flash which isolates them, happily illumined against the black ground, the photographer fails to record that I am waiting in the darkness. The photo is part of me, though I can't recall it. My memory depends on this black hole in time, an unknowable moment at which the collection comes together, becomes the record of another sort of memory: that of my family. This moment on the bridge is in fact the transition from one experience of my photographic collection to another. It captures the coming together of the two strands of images with which I cannot connect myself and can only, by the most strenuous act of concentration, catch brief glimpses of the tender actuality of these two people. Here, however, they loom into view with an insistence which says: we are your past. This is not merely a moment in time captured, or frozen into monochrome. It is also a bridge between a distant past and my own.

¶ *Time before time*

St Augustine was the first writer to look back on his childhood and experience this sense of vertigo while trying to reconstitute a lost self. In his *Confessions*, Augustine essayed the first proper autobiography in the history of Western literature. Others had recounted the stories of their own lives from a first-person perspective, but Augustine deserves the title of inaugural autobiographer because, for him, the very notion of a self presents so many problems for the author who wishes to trace the development of his adult personality. Augustine knows that a book about himself must also be a book about time: a book in which time is not a current flowing in a single direction, but a dizzy confusion of eddies and undertows. The *Confessions* stage the author's dramatic struggle to make the mad flux of time settle into serene channels, to navigate between past and present in order to reach the shores of future redemption.

His problems begin almost at once. In his opening chapter, Augustine attempts to recall his earliest memories, to imagine himself back into the self he had once been. It is, he quickly discovers, an excruciating task. At what point, he wonders, can he truly be said to have become himself? Not, he complains, at his conception, for he has no memory of the time he spent in his mother's womb. At his birth, then? Not quite. He certainly existed, he writes, but how can he connect his adult self with the infant whose consciousness is lost to time? 'Thus, Lord,' he writes,

> I do not remember living this age of my infancy; I must take the word of others about it and can only conjecture how I spent it – even if with a fair amount of certainty – from watching others now in the same stage. I am

loth, indeed, to count it as part of the life I live in this world. For it is buried in the darkness of the forgotten as completely as the period earlier still that I spent in my mother's womb.

Augustine imagines a time before language, and therefore, he says, a time before himself. In a terrifying confusion which turns out to be the philosophical heart of Augustine's doubt (about the possibility of his redemption in and by God), birth and death appear to coincide: they are both moments on which the continuum of a life depends, but both are entirely mysterious, twin voids at either end of existence, supporting between them a time which ceases to have meaning if we concede their meaninglessness. Their mirrored terror resides in the fact that there has existed (and will exist again) a time in which 'I' do not exist. But the first mystery is somehow even more unsettling than the second. Death, of course, we can do nothing about; but our origins are subject to the most painful entreaties. We peer back into the darkness of the past, convinced that there must be some evidence there of our own future being. And we find, according to Augustine's doleful reflections, nothing. We seem to have stumbled on to the stage of our own lives before the curtain has come up.

The advent of photography has at least illuminated for us that uncertain realm of infancy. But it has had the effect too of making the ghosts that we once were persist in a way that might previously have been dispersed in the intricacies and uncertainties of storytelling. Augustine is partly comforted by the stories told of his own infancy; he knows that he gradually emerged from this mute, apparently unthinking state to speak and act in ways that he can remember. Photographs of ourselves as infants thrust us back into an Augustinian unease: here we are faced with the evidence of the being we most certainly once were, but can never recall.

In the opening pages of his autobiographical *Speak, Memory*, Vladimir Nabokov imagines two apparently contrasting moments: one of them filmed, the other, though unrecorded, an image which has all the mnemonic potential of a photograph, but which has left no evidence other than the author's exquisite reconstruction of it. *Speak, Memory*, claims the book's subtitle, is 'an autobiography revisited': as if the act of recalling the past were always a matter of recapitulating a reality already remembered elsewhere, at other times. It may be – although Nabokov doesn't admit it – that he is disguising his own fearful reading of a family relic when he writes:

> I know, however, of a young chronophobiac who experienced something like panic when looking for the first time at homemade movies that had been taken a few weeks before his birth. He saw a world that was practically unchanged – the same house, the same people – and then realized that he did not exist there at all and that nobody mourned his absence. He caught a glimpse of his mother waving from an upstairs window, and that unfamiliar gesture disturbed him, as if it were some mysterious farewell. But what particularly frightened him was the sight of a brand-new baby carriage standing there on the porch, with the smug, encroaching air of a coffin; even that was empty, as if, in the reverse course of events, his very bones had disintegrated.

The image provides plentiful evidence of his future existence – the house, his mother, the baby carriage – but the object (himself) which ought to mark its centre is entirely absent. This horrifically vacant tableau is contrasted, for Nabokov, with the founding image in his own memorial archive. He recalls a moment – unphotographed but very like the perfect family portrait – at which he claims to have become aware, for the first time, of his own place in the temporal scheme of things. He pictures himself, aged four, strolling happily between his mother and father:

> I felt myself plunged abruptly into a radiant and mobile medium that was nothing other than the pure element of time. One shared it – just as excited bathers share shining seawater – with creatures that were not oneself but that were joined to one by time's common flow, an environment quite different from the spatial world, which not only man but apes and butterflies can perceive. At that instant, I became acutely aware that the twenty-seven-year-old being, in soft white and pink, holding my left hand, was my mother, and that the thirty-three-year-old being, in hard white and gold, holding my right hand, was my father. Between them, as they evenly progressed, I strutted, and trotted, and strutted again, from sun fleck to sun fleck, which I easily identify today with an alley of ornamental oaklings in the park of our country estate, Vyra, in the former Province of St Petersburg, Russia.

The child feels himself suddenly to have succeeded in parsing an equation whose terms are the relative ages of himself and his parents, and whose logic is assured by their moving together along the path. He finds himself to be the overlapping, shaded-in space between several sets of temporal elements: his mother's gauzy beauty, his father's military career (long past: he is wearing the gilt trappings of his former regiment 'as a festive joke'), the slow time of the estate where they are walking (soon to be accelerated, then curtailed, by revolution: the young Vladimir will never see those oaklings become mature trees). The scene is idyllic, but its details begin to hint at their own passing; the instant of the author's 'birth of sentient life' is also the moment when he becomes fretfully aware of chronology and decay: 'for several years afterward I remained keenly interested in the age of my parents and kept myself informed about it, like a nervous passenger asking the time in order to check a new watch'. In a way, he is as absent from this formative image of his family as the young man who is unsettled by the filmed evidence of his own paradoxically prenatal after-life. The family 'photograph' which this second passage describes is equally, despite the cheerful four-year-old at its centre, a rather melancholy picture of a world evacuated of meaning.

The photograph which seems most precisely to register the condition of my own palpably present non-being (my not-yetness, the tardy shadow of my arrival in the world) is not actually the first snapshot in which I appear. There are other, earlier images in which I see myself as a black and white bundle in the arms of a few delighted and solicitous adults. We are all rather blurred: my parents, no doubt, are exhausted by the new arrival (by all accounts I was an exceptionally noisy baby, screaming my way through the first year, then promptly shutting up for the next eighteen). Here I am in the summer of 1969, held aloft by the youngest of my mother's sisters. I'm not yet recognizable, but I seem to be able to identify with this tiny grey mass. As also with another photograph, taken perhaps a year later in the garden of my father's parents' house. Here, I'm held by both grandparents in an unconvincing imitation of an already walking infant.

These photographs fail to touch me like another, in which I am seated, a brown blob, on the weeds of our back garden. With one hand, I clutch at my father's side as he half squats, half kneels with my brother Paul in his arms. Paul is a few months old; it is the summer of 1970. Behind us, the leaves of a flourishing lilac bush are edged with yellow, a few of them burnt brown (by late summer heat or the onset of autumn, it is impossible to say).

Perhaps the photograph looks like such an image of happiness because it has been taken by my mother. It dates from a time before she had begun to resent the camera's materialization on a summer afternoon, before her own image of herself cracked and faded to the point where she could no longer bear to be photographed. She must have felt as if the camera itself were punishing her, the photograph repeating the process of hardening, the tightening of her skin, her slow shrinking into what she must have thought of as a desiccated version of herself, of the youthful person in the other photographs. And did she picture this unphotographable version of herself, without pain, without the visual markers of her decline? I imagine that if I were in her place I would be racked by images of myself as I might have been: whole, easy, free. And did she remember the feeling of being photographed knowing she had a body whole and ready to shine out in the image as itself, and not as this other version of herself? In a photo of my brother Paul's confirmation, she edges out of the frame, and I can almost recall her entreaties to my father's sister not to photograph her.

¶ *'Widower with sons'*

The years between this photograph and my father's death nearly a decade later are, in terms of the family photo archive, almost totally invisible. Only a single photograph, taken a matter of weeks before my mother died, interrupts the void. I had always known that this gap sat at the heart of my collection. In fact, I think I had already felt the absence of visual record of my own life, and that of my family, as a strange, eccentric lack. I remember feeling that this disappearance of the camera from our lives a vanishing I would look back on in later life; I was not sure if I would regret it. I certainly noticed it again after my mother's death: I began to get used to the fact that my adolescence was entirely undocumented. In early adulthood, after my father's death, I could even joke about this, counting myself lucky that no record existed of various disasters of dress and hairstyle, nor of the endless eruptions of my skin. But by the time I looked at these photographs again, weakened by depression, the sudden leap across years had come to seem especially significant.

I tried to imagine what photographs of that period in our lives might have looked like. How would we have faced the camera in the months before my mother died? Was it possible that we might have passed ourselves off as a normal family? How clearly would my mother's symptoms have been represented there? How vividly would the strain on my father's face have shown? How adequately might I have been able to mask the mixture of shame, fear and anger that I felt? I wondered, in other words, what we must have looked like from the outside. Might my father, my brothers and I, in the months and years after my mother's death, have revealed in our appearance some aspect specific to a family bereft of a wife and mother? I could not picture those four figures, though I thought I might have discerned something of our awkward gathering around this absence in a photograph taken in 1914 by August Sander. The image is entitled 'Widower with sons'. The squat widower is photographed in his parlour. He looks perhaps modestly prosperous, sombrely gazing away from the camera, his arms loosely around his two sons. The elder son looks at the camera openly, quizzically; the younger more tentatively, his gaze slightly blurred. Their heads are shaved, and they are dressed identically in faintly rumpled shirts with large round collars and shorts that come just below their knees. They are aged, maybe, fourteen and twelve, but it is difficult to tell: the first striking thing about their appearance is that they are too old for these clothes. Not only are their shirt sleeves too short, but their clothes seem ancient, too scuffed to be quite suitable for this curtailed family portrait, this stranded trio for whom the family snapshot can only bring to mind the absent mother. These details suggest a frail effort to hang on to the realm of familial appearance, the idea of a visual index that announces their togetherness in the face of bereavement. The Widower is defined only by his loss, a loss that spreads itself over the surface of a photograph which declares: there will be no more family portraits except as images of that loss. Had we been photographed, I thought, we might have looked like Sander's dismal grouping: we would have been the iconic presentment of bereavement, but also of the failure of the bereft to find a way of addressing their loss.

¶ *Last things*

During those long evenings when I stared at these photographs, there was one which I used regularly to let slip to the bottom of the pile unexamined. I found it almost impossible to look at it for long. The final photograph of my parents was taken in the early summer of 1985, some weeks before my mother died. It is also the last image I have of my father; there were no more family photographs, and I have no idea what became of my parents' camera in the five years between their deaths. In fact, it may already have vanished, been hidden away where it could no longer remind us of a time when we had faced it without dread. This photograph, before me now, was taken by my father's sister, in the living room of her house, five minutes' walk from ours. It was, I think, a Sunday afternoon, and my parents had gone, as usual, to see my aunt: this time without my brothers or me, who would all have been preparing for (or perhaps already in the middle of) school exams. I can trace no other photographs from the same occasion, so I must assume that my aunt passed this one on as the sole example of an image which would by this time have become noticeable by its rarity. I have no way of telling when she might have handed it over: whether it joined the rest of our familial photographic collection before or after my mother died. If the latter, then my aunt must, I assume, have given it to my father much later, in the knowledge that it was not only the last photograph of my mother, but a unique reminder of how she looked towards the end of her life.

It was already some years since we had given up taking photographs, and I can imagine that as my aunt produced her camera that afternoon, my mother would have protested. I cannot blame my aunt for insisting on taking this picture; we might all have grown used to my mother's objections to having her photograph taken, but I don't think we quite understood the extent of her discomfort. Captured for the last time beside her, however, my father clearly knows the degree of that pain and reticence, her sense of being exposed to a vision that recorded too clearly the evidence of her decline. She has recently been in and out of hospital for months, as several of her symptoms worsen and require interventions which, here, she has done her best to hide.

My parents are sitting in the corner of the room, side by side on a pair of ancient and, I recall, extremely uncomfortable armchairs that have been pushed together so that they are close enough for my father to put his right arm round my mother's shoulders. His hand stretches towards her upper arm, but only his fingertips rest on the fabric of her blouse, as if any more insistent touch might injure her frail body. But also, the gesture is quite unfamiliar to me; there is only one other photograph in which he reaches out to her like this. My father sits stiffly back in his chair: I have the impression that he too is ill at ease with this now unaccustomed ritual of the photograph. His faint smile is a touch too strained; he looks as though he has had to will himself to project even this modest sign of assurance before the camera. Although I know that he is not yet aware of the precise seriousness of my mother's current condition, I cannot help wondering if he has guessed that this will be their last photograph together. That certainty, I know, is for him only a matter of days away.

My mother, too, is attempting to smile. Her discomfort is more obvious; even this slight movement of her features has revealed the stiffness of her face: the lines around her mouth that have in recent years been for her the most visible signs of her disease. Or rather, amongst all the symptoms that have assailed her, this has been the one which she would focus on when faced with a camera. She insisted at such moments that she could not let herself be photographed looking, as she thought, so much older than her years. At the time, I could not see the disparity that so disturbed her; now, looking at this photograph again, I can see that she looks considerably older than fifty (the photograph would have been taken a few weeks after her birthday). But the more insidious and dangerous attack on her body is taking place elsewhere, in an acceleration of all the symptoms that have slowly debilitated her over the years, joined now by invisible but (as my father will soon be informed) definitive and irreversible developments. She has crossed her arms so that her left hand is hidden beneath her right elbow. She is concealing a bandaged finger from the camera. The circulation in her hands has got so weak that the tissue has begun to perish. Sometime in the next few weeks, she will have this fingernail removed: otherwise, she will be told, gangrene is likely to set in. Still, this is not the worst of her agonies. Her slim figure has shrunk to an emaciated shadow: her throat has contracted and she finds it horrifyingly painful to eat. Meals have become, for all of us, ordeals of vigilance and intermittent panic, as she is in danger of choking on the smallest morsel.

Here, in the photograph, she is even frailer than I recall. And I am amazed, given how thin and ill she looks, that she retains just enough of the poise that sets her apart in the earlier photographs I own, to rise briefly above her failing body and face the camera with a dignity I know, in her situation, I could not possibly discover.

I cannot look at this image without relating it to the photograph, taken perhaps twenty-five years earlier, of my parents crossing O'Connell Bridge. It is not merely that these are the only two photographs in which they appear alone together. For years, I now realize, I gazed at that earlier photograph in order to avoid looking at this one. I mythologized it, turning it into an emblem of what I had lost, when really (and I knew this, dimly, each time I passed over the last photograph in favour of the first) the truth I was looking for was here, in the vision I could not bear to contemplate because it seemed so brutal, so obvious a reminder. Now, in their twin evocation of an intimacy I can find nowhere else, the two pictures seem to stand out and frame the rest. But more than that, they return me to the essential mystery of the whole collection: that here, in the paired gazes of my parents, I fail to discern what future they are, together, facing. The photographs (all photographs) say to us that their subjects are alive and dead at the same time. I look at my mother's face and think: she is dead, and she is going to die. But what I cannot find there is a hint of what she might see in front of her. This is the terror that I could not face in the years when I refused to look at this photograph: the feeling that that future was entirely open, that the hopes or fears I might imagine I had caught sight of there were unverifiable. With the first photograph, my own existence was hanging in the balance; with this one (a much more fearful conjecture) everything was both certain and atrociously unfathomable at the same time. I look at this photograph and can hardly bear the real presence I find there; for it fails to settle into the consoling, monochrome distance of the period photograph. It is still palpably present, too tangible, too physical.

BODIES

'There was scarcely anything left of body or mind
by which one could say "This is he" or "This is she".
Sometimes a hand was raised as if to clutch something
or ward off something or somebody groaned, or
somebody laughed aloud as if sharing a joke with
nothingness.'
— Virginia Woolf, *To the Lighthouse*

'The way I keep in touch with the world is very
gingerly, because the world touches too hard.'
— Don Van Vliet

In the last photograph of my parents, taken a few weeks before my mother died, I thought I had discovered the image of her that was both the full stop to a life and the capital that set a coded sentence in backward motion, into the past, where I might recompose a story that ended there: in muted colours on a Sunday afternoon as my father's hand reached out gently to rest on her shoulder. But in truth, it is only the last image before the last: there is another picture waiting for me in a place I hesitate to revisit. The photographs seem to baulk and stumble before this final hurdle, a memorial suffix I must, despite my reticence, attempt to append. The image I am thinking of now is unphotographed, but also so frozen in my memory that I can register it only as a silent tableau, a distant and static moment, emulsified by regret. It is actually the last image of my mother which I can call to mind, and perhaps it is so difficult to focus on it because it demands that I step outside the series of frozen photographic moments and into another time: the time of real loss.

There is something intolerably abstract about the language of funerals, a grim syntax that depends on adding a spurious and abstract definite article to actions which are horribly physical: the memorial, the service, the burial. Of these, 'the viewing' is surely the least honest or accurate: a phrase that seems, euphemistically, to defuse a terrible reality and at the same time to turn it into a grotesque spectacle. By what ruse of word and thought do we transmute our being in the presence of the dead into an experience merely of seeing? What desire is answered by this transformation of death's physicality into a purely visual event? And what do we imagine, faced with this vision, that we are trying to remember, or to forget? The body? A ceremony? Memory itself? There are funerary traditions whereby it is apparently quite normal to photograph, even to film the proceedings: but on the day that I am now trying to picture, such rituals would have been unthinkable. Instead, I recall only this dreadfully circumscribed and labelled act of seeing.

'The viewing' was quite unexpected. I'm certain that nobody had explained to me the morning's itinerary, or even hinted that the car which arrived too early for my half-awake body would take us not straight to the nearby church but to the hospital where my mother's body still lay. I remember clearly a moment of realization as the car turned in the wrong direction, and the passing streets began to look quite unreal, the morning shoppers who turned to look at the car almost comical in their double-takes, looking for a hearse and a body that weren't there. The journey was soundtracked in my head by the idiot chorus of a song that I loathed ('Shout! Shout! Let it all out!') but that at least allowed me, for those hushed minutes in the car, to find an object for my anger, fear and embarrassment other than the scene I came, in slow panic, to realize was waiting for me in a mortuary room at the end of the journey.

A photograph of that room, taken from my point of view, would have been mostly a perplex of shadows, a confusion of lurking and indistinct bodies whose outlines I cannot picture at all. Nor do I remember the prayers which must have been voiced, or the responses of the mourners to a priest (my mother's cousin) whose authority assured them of an order, a ceremony, taken, thankfully, out of their hands. I remember only what I did not want to see: an open coffin at the centre of the room, and my mother's face. There is only this one point of light, condensed around a being who has become, in fact, only a face. This is what we are here to view.

Do we ever truly see, or remember, the corpse of a loved one? It seems to me that on that morning, stranded in a glum adjunct of the hospital where my mother's life had ended a few days before, we were gathered not around a body but before a face. The face is perhaps as much of a reminder as we can bear: the failed body safely hidden and adorned, except, I think, for my mother's hands, which I can no longer see but which a more abstract memory tells me were clasped above her, holding a rosary. The face, we tell ourselves, is as if sleeping. What do we hope to find there? I don't believe that my stunned sixteen-year-old mind, on that July morning, was subject to this speculation, but I do recall that as I looked at my mother's coffin my gaze seemed to fracture. And at the same time I knew that what I was looking at – this face which did indeed (the cliché was true) look as if it were sleeping – was about to become an image in my memory. Was that why we were there: to be able, later, to remember this moment of remembering? The thought was unnerving, discomposing, and I remember that at that instant I felt that I had let my mother down, had failed (just as I neglected, on that day and for many years afterwards, to weep for her) to live up to the kind of memorial ritual which she herself had recently described.

I remembered my mother returning home from the funeral of an aunt and describing the old woman's face: a face, she said, from which the years had fallen away. At the time, I had been secretly appalled by the thought of my mother's gaze on the body of her dead aunt, quite unable to imagine a state of mind for which a corpse could be anything other than an image of physical horror and mortal fear. I had never seen the faces of my dead grandmothers, and cannot now recall whether I saw the corpse of my father's father eight months before my mother died. Looking at her face now, I simply did not want to remember what I was seeing. I spent the day trying hard not to let the sights that assailed me impinge, to become the kind of spectacle of which I might one day say that my mother had looked, in her coffin, young again.

So conventional is the observation of death's strangely rejuvenating effect on the faces of the deceased that it is almost a disappointment to come across it in the pages of Proust, a writer so alive to the intricacies of mourning. We have already seen him make a link between photography and death; here, however, is its intimate, detailed expression. The narrator, after a long absence, returns, unannounced, to the drawing room of his grandmother. Instead of the beloved grandmother of his memory, he sees, 'sitting on the sofa, beneath the lamp, red-faced, heavy and common, sick, lost in thought, following the lines of a book with eyes that seemed hardly sane, a dejected old woman whom I did not know'. He immediately compares this terrifying vision of his grandmother with a photograph, as the antithesis of a scene charged with familiarity, intimacy and memory:

> Of myself – thanks to that privilege which does not last
> but which gives one, during the brief moment of return,
> the faculty of being suddenly the spectator of one's
> own absence – there was present only the witness, the
> observer, in travelling coat and hat, the stranger who does
> not belong to the house, the photographer who has called
> to take a photograph of places which one will never see
> again.

Marcel's grandmother looks like a photograph precisely because she no longer accords with the image of her in his memory, and also because it is obvious from this scene that confronts him that she is going to die. The grandmother suddenly occupies a pure present and is therefore fated to pass from that present into death.

An hour or two after the grandmother's death, the family servant, Françoise, combs her hair, which had always seemed less old than her face,

> only tinged with grey. ... But now, on the contrary, it alone set the crown of age on a face grown young again, from which had vanished the wrinkles, the contractions, the swellings, the strains, the hollows which pain had carved on it over the years. ... Life in withdrawing from her had taken with it the disillusionments of life. A smile seemed to be hovering on my grandmother's lips. On that funeral couch, death, like a sculptor of the Middle Ages, had laid her down in the form of a young girl.

The vision of his grandmother as a young girl is, of course, an image that Marcel has never actually seen: her dead face shows him not his own memory of her but an imagined face (or perhaps, yet again, the face of an old photograph). The dead face lures him into a time in which he does not belong.

We might conclude from this passage that the memorial scene I am trying to describe is a treacherous one: the face of the deceased drags us back into an uncertain, unverifiable experience of time. But it shoves us forward too, into a future in which we know the image before us will itself furnish further memories, possibly just as unreliable. When I ask myself if I really saw the dead body of my mother in the mortuary of a Dublin hospital in

July 1985, the question is not a historical one. I know I was there; but what exactly did I see? My most vivid memory is the violent certainty that I was seeing all the wrong things, that I was incapable of bearing the weight of the memories that pressed down on me like the mortuary's low ceiling.

I was already terrified of what I might remember. A few days earlier, my father, my brothers and I had been hurried, on arriving at the hospital in the early morning, to the room where my mother was dying. My father spoke to her quietly, telling her that 'the boys' were there, and I am sure that for a moment (though a nurse told us she was unconscious) she opened her eyes. The nurse led my brothers and me to a waiting room, where my father's sister, perhaps a silent hour later, asked us if we wanted to go back to see my mother again. Or rather, she asked me; and I said no. My aunt assured me: 'You can remember...' I wondered what I was supposed to remember. Later, around midday, one of my mother's sisters came to the nearby pub where an uncle had taken us to eat, and said: 'She's gone.'

And so I have no memory of my mother's death. Instead I recall these adjacent images, fragments of an experience I was already trying not to remember. Out of the gloom of the mortuary – which may very well have been brightly lit; I remember no more than the patch of light at its centre – only two images loom with any real clarity. At some stage in the proceedings, there opens an expanse of silence out of which my father moves towards my mother's body. He kisses her face and, turning, gestures me towards the coffin. I have, at that moment, absolutely no idea what to do. I move towards my mother and lean over the edge of the coffin to kiss her cheek. But I am quite unsure whether that is what is required of me.

I don't remember the kiss at all, only this: the feeling that I am at the centre of some vast geometry of embarrassment, that a crowd of vigilant shadows surrounds me. I am gripped by the awful suspicion that if I have done the wrong thing (perhaps my father simply wanted me to join him beside the coffin), my brothers will follow my lead, and we will have performed a dreadful – macabre, unnecessarily demonstrative – action, a gesture quite spontaneous for my father but somehow overwrought and out of place for his sons. I have no notion what my place is in this unexpected ritual, no idea how to behave before a body which seems a reminder only of my distance from my mother's death. And so my most lasting impression of that moment is one of unconquerable shame.

The priest intones a final prayer before the coffin is closed. Again the scene is vague and shadowed in my memory, but for the blaze of white about my mother's face. Into that paleness at the centre of the picture, there intrudes a tiny black dot. A fly buzzes around my mother's head. And then, a gesture: my grandfather's arm moves into the shot, waves the insect away. But the fly is tenacious; it returns, lands lightly on my mother's cheek, and again her father brushes it off. The whole picture seems to stiffen around these movements, repeated as my grandfather becomes more agitated, begins to cry, becomes the single awkwardly mobile figure in the stillness of the room. The image is both unbearable and strangely distant; at that moment I can think of nothing but that this is what I will remember of my last glimpse of my mother: an old man desperately trying to protect his daughter's body. I remember thinking how unreal this image was, how it looked already as if the moment had been excised from a fiction, a cinematic cliché as

176

remote from the reality of my mother's dead body as my own giddy and wavering perspective.

I seem only to recall images of this distance, to remember the gulf between my mother's body and me, my failure to see it, to see her, as a proper reminder of who she had been. The whole day seems a series of cracked images of this misrecognition, of the severing of my body from an authentic remembrance or mourning. Later, at the church, another of the officiating priests would approach the pew where we sat and ask which of the three of us was Brian: the one, he had been told, who looked most like my father. He seemed not to be able to see me, and my sense that I was not really part of this scene at all was only heightened when my father joked that he must want to speak to 'the good-looking one'. The poor priest was none the wiser. It was as if the familiar network of family likenesses had broken down, and I could no longer rely on my resemblance to my father. And if I had begun, in adolescence, to resent the frequent remarking of this likeness, it now seemed the marker of a physical memory in the process of being undone. In fact, I felt that I was no longer able to recognize the bodies around me, nor to make them remain solidly in their own time: at least three bodies seemed to meet in the image of my mother's corpse. The corpse, a reminder of the living body, returns us to our own remembering body. Together, they make a frieze that is subject to the violent amputations of forgetting and the aching reminder of bodies long gone.

¶ *The forefinger*

I am trying to picture again my mother in her coffin, trying to clear the fog that surrounds the singular clarity of her face, to see more of that scene than is given to me by my recollection of the moment of the kiss and my grandfather's awkwardly advancing, stricken hand. But the effort is fruitless: time and again I fail to see the rest of her: I cannot see her hands. This absence is quite at odds with my memory of her when, in the last years of her life, so much of her presence depended on the condition of her hands. What exactly is it that I cannot recall there, where there ought to be a lucid picture of the body I knew so well?

In the second chapter of *David Copperfield* – a chapter simply entitled 'I observe' – Dickens has his hero sketch for the reader a few of his earliest impressions:

> The first objects that assume a distinct presence before me, as I look far back, into the blank of my infancy, are my mother with her pretty hair and youthful shape, and [the servant] Peggotty with no shape at all, and eyes so dark that they seemed to darken their whole neighbourhood in her face, and cheeks and arms so hard and red that I wondered the birds didn't peck her in preference to apples.
>
> I believe I can remember these two at a little distance apart, dwarfed to my sight by stooping down or kneeling on the floor, and I going unsteadily from one to the other. I have an impression on my mind which I cannot distinguish from actual remembrance, of the touch of Peggotty's forefinger as she used to hold it out to me, and of its being roughened by needlework, like a pocket nutmeg-grater.

David is unsure of the accuracy of his memory: 'this may be fancy', he concedes. But the luminousness of the image is enough at least to convince us that, plausible or not, the reanimated scene has stayed with David Copperfield, and has nourished his later life in ways, as he says, that have made him capable of being happy. It is only, he reflects, those who can remember such details who are able 'to retain a certain freshness, and gentleness, and capacity of being pleased'. David's ability to recall these moments (or, perhaps, to invent them) is enough – or so Dickens would have us believe, at this early juncture in his novel – to convince the reader of the narrator's reliability.

But the most striking moment in this briefly fancied recollection is surely the tiny detail of Peggotty's forefinger. It is the one aspect of the remembered moment that is not visual but tactile. David (or Dickens) remembers, first of all, the touch of an adult hand. The child is astonished by the roughness of the adult's finger, as if he cannot quite believe that this unyielding skin was once as pliable and youthful as his own. To the child, no other part of the adult's body is so alien. Everything else – height, bulk, grey hairs and deep lines – is as yet too far away to impress anything of the sense of time having hardened around the ageing body. I have a very clear memory of my father's hands. Their weathered asperity looked to me to inhabit a world of maturity and confidence of which I would never be a part. I remember this thought: my father's hands must be less capable than my own of really feeling what they touched. If I felt too that I could never fit myself to that second skin, it must have been because, despite the tradition of my resemblance to my father, I had already identified my own body with the texture of my mother's hands.

This affinity was rarely made tangible by touch: I have no memory of holding my mother's hand. A single photograph records a moment in a park sometime in the mid-1970s when it seems I did actually clasp her hand (perhaps only for the camera?), but my memory of her is dominated by the condition of her hands, and the photograph serves only to make me wonder if the hand I am holding there is already the hand I remember. The symptoms must have arrived slowly, almost imperceptibly, her new sensitivity to the cold giving no clue to the pain that would later, by a horrible paradox, separate her from the touch of the world around her at the same time as it sealed her body in an unbearable sensitivity. I remember an eventual diagnosis: Raynaud's syndrome, an inherited circulatory disorder which, it turned out, afflicted several members of her family. It must have seemed at first a mere annoyance. She needed to wear gloves well into spring, to avoid immersing her hands in even tepid water (we acquired a dishwasher), to have her fingers regularly massaged back from the blue edge of advancing cold (a touch I do recall). I remember that I became accustomed, on wintry afternoons and then in warmer seasons, to shopping trips in search of warmer gloves and, later, of fleeced boots chosen from catalogues that arrived regularly in the post.

I can only imagine how my mother's gradual retreat from health must have felt. As I remember it, there was no sudden plunge into sickness, just this protracted drift away from the shores of ease with the world and into icy currents of pain. I can piece together only the flimsiest of chronologies: I know that her hands suffered first, and that one summer, on returning from our usual holiday at her father's house in Kerry, she noticed that some patches of skin on her neck and chest were untanned.

I can picture her now, standing in front of the big mirror in her room, examining these peculiar blotches, but I can no longer tell whether this image derives from a time before or after the diagnosis that would set her on an uncertain course.

Sickness is a kind of time travel. It does fearsome, paradoxical things to our sense of chronology, tipping us into an alternate time which seems to accelerate, dizzyingly, or to slow to a geological crawl, setting us apart, as if airlocked, from the world around us. The poet John Donne, having recovered, in 1624, from a long and life-threatening sickness, wrote of this plunge into a painfully personal time:

> Variable, and therefore miserable, condition of man! this
> minute I was well, and am ill, this minute. I am surprised
> with a sudden change, and alteration to worse, and can
> impute it to no cause, nor call it by any name. We study
> health, and we deliberate upon our meats, and drink,
> and air, and exercises, and we hew and we polish every
> stone that goes to that building; and so our health is a long
> and a regular work: but in a minute a cannon batters all,
> overthrows all, demolishes all; a sickness unprevented for
> all our diligence, unsuspected for all our curiosity; nay,
> undeserved, if we consider only disorder, summons us,
> seizes us, possesses us, destroys us in an instant.

I wonder now if my mother lived through such a moment. If so, I never saw it for what it was. It was only later that I remembered her returning from a hospital appointment and telling my father her diagnosis: a rare autoimmune disease called scleroderma (I became so familiar with the word that it was only years after she died that I stopped to think of its Latinate meaning). Even then, perhaps a diagnosis was not, in her mind, such a terrible blow. The symptoms were disturbing but not as yet crippling, and perhaps for a time there was at least a sense that in naming her illness she had begun to accommodate herself to it. I remember this much of what she told my father: that the disease would tighten and discolour her skin. She grew accustomed to the comments of neighbours and friends who thought she looked very well; what looked like a healthy tan was in fact evidence that the disease had taken hold of her whole body. And I remember this: her doctors' assurance that, although the disease was incurable, and would slowly debilitate her, it would not kill her.

Scleroderma, it is true, is not always, or often, fatal. Of its two varieties – 'limited' and 'diffuse' – the first, while debilitating, painful and disfiguring, is more in the order of a manageable, chronic condition than a life-threatening disease. And even the second is unpredictable, the patient's prognosis depending largely on events in the first few years after diagnosis, when the illness usually announces its long-term intent by the presence or absence of damage to the internal organs. The name 'scleroderma' – denoting, in recognition of the most obvious effect of the disease, a simple hardening of the skin – was given to a set of symptoms in the middle of the nineteenth century, but the first recorded case seems to be that of a seventeen-year-old girl in Naples in 1752. Carlo Curzio, a physician at the city's Royal Hospital, recorded, the following year, that the girl had come to him barely able to open her mouth or move her head, so hard and tight had her skin become. Curzio prescribed warm milk, vapour baths, bleeding of the foot and small doses of mercury; after eleven months of these treatments, he writes, his patient's skin had returned to its former suppleness. Reading modern accounts of the myriad tortures which scleroderma inflicts upon its victims (its later title of 'systemic sclerosis' is closer to the reality of a disease which merely announces itself on the skin), I wonder what became of this poor girl. If Curzio is indeed the first to describe the disease that killed my mother in a few short years, this cannot have been the end of her suffering.

Scleroderma is incurable and, in its origins, enigmatic. Some connection to physical or emotional trauma has recently been conjectured. The mechanism by which it wreaks havoc in almost every part of the body has been isolated – a generalized build-up of collagen in the body's connective tissues – but this hints, for the layperson, at few of its atrocious effects, and, for the specialist, at not many more of its possible causes. The list of symptoms (a list I don't need to read) is almost incredible in its extravagance, in the insidiousness with which the disease infiltrates every interstice of the patient's body. Its visible portents are also its first agonies: it is prefaced by the slow onset of Raynaud's syndrome, a not uncommon affliction by which the hands, when subjected to cold, turn white, then blue. (More than one generation of my mother's family exhibits these signs; every winter, I pay close attention to the numbness of my fingers, waiting for my turn.) There follows a thickening of the skin which may be confined or diffused about the body: the skin hardens, becoming shiny and impermeable (pores close, hair follicles are destroyed). At this point in its progression, the disease can be most distressing simply in its alarming effects on the face. The patient, it is said, feels as if she were being given a slow facelift. But the process continues until the face has not merely tightened, but noticeably altered in shape. Experts have offered the grotesque term *Mauskopf* to denote this new and, for the patient, terrifyingly alien face, which looks as though it were being pinched, contracting around the nose and mouth. The face, in fact, becomes a mask: lips, nose, eyelids and cheeks all lose their mobility; speech becomes difficult, and eating more so, as the mouth shrinks and sharp lines are incised around the lips. Later, the newly impassive face may be marked by deep lesions, typically extending vertically down the forehead. Again, the terminology is appalling: this stage is given the far too vivid name of 'scleroderma *en coup de sabre*', as if the victim's face has literally been lacerated by the blow of a sword. Eventually, once the disease has entered what is called its 'atrophic' stage, the skin relaxes once again; but it now begins to be marked by patches of ruined blood vessels, which manifest almost symmetrically, composing a 'butterfly' effect.

Such symptoms are only the beginning. In turn, all major organs are attacked directly (except, as if by some wretchedly poetic irony, the heart, which suffers only as a result of ravages elsewhere). The oesophagus contracts and becomes rigid, taking on – so the literature has it – the appearance of a solid 'glass tube'. What little food the patient can swallow causes an excruciating acid reflux, leading to further scarring. The intestines cease to absorb nutrients efficiently. All of this leads to pronounced weight loss. The lungs are subject to a stealthy fibrosis, so that the patient is exhausted and breathless after the slightest exertion. (Scleroderma has unfathomable affinities with the occupational diseases of miners and those who have worked with and been poisoned by solvents and pesticides.) The salivary glands come under attack, leaving the patient permanently dry-mouthed, making speech even more uncomfortable. Muscles begin to waste, joints to stiffen and bone to produce excrescences. Calcified, bone-like deposits appear beneath the skin, threatening and disfiguring its surface further as they break through. At last, as happened to my mother, the kidneys start to fail: this is what kills most of those who die from scleroderma.

Of this comprehensive and horrific array of symptoms, the one that haunts me most is the effect of the disease on the patient's hands, for this was the pain of which my mother complained most, and the debility that seemed, to me at least, to cause her the greatest frustration. Her hands gradually became useless: blood flow was cut off, the skin became as hard as wood, and vicious sores and infections erupted in her fingertips to remind her that she still, despite her body's hardening against the world, had feeling there. She wore gloves when leaving the house, no longer only to protect her already ailing hands against the cold, but to avoid comment on the sight of her fingers turning inwards to form (as, once more, the medical accounts I have read put it with, for me, an unwarranted precision) a pair of immobile claws. She baulked, I remember, at the clumsy remedies to which she was invited to resort to help her carry out the simplest tasks. Sometime in the last couple of years of her life, she purchased a pair of electrically heated gloves that attached to a heavy rechargeable battery. I think she rarely used this awkward technology, and resisted to the end a dismal catalogue of utensils designed for the use of the aged, infirm or arthritic. She must have wanted to maintain at least the illusion that she could reach out to the world of her own accord, although every touch, every effort to make contact with the things or bodies around her was a reminder of how she had retreated from that world.

My mother's case, as a doctor once informed her, was the worst (the most aggressive, the most rapidly advancing, the least responsive to treatment) that the several specialists who attended to her diverse sufferings had ever come across. What little they could do for her by way of alleviating specific symptoms had, on occasion, even more debilitating effects. In the last year of her life, one drug caused such a rapid depletion of potassium in her body that she ended up in a psychiatric ward. I was old enough to know that this was a particular cruelty of the disease: to have subjected her to the keenest degree of a pain with which she was already too familiar. For

years, she had fought against a depression that, as I recall it, predated her physical illness by several years (I
have the vaguest recollection that I knew there might be
some connection between the two: the mysterious origin of the disease in the body's response to trauma or
distress must already have been suspected). Her depression had come and gone like a malign sort of weather. It
engulfs, or recedes from, many of my childhood memories, hovering as an indistinct pressure at the edges of
my recollection of specific times, or spiralling to enclose
a very clear image: for instance, her endless round of
medications, of which the then current and mostly useless recourse to crude tranquillizers is the most vivid in
my memory: a profusion of little green pills that, long
after she died, still turned up sometimes in dusty drawers and cabinets.

One of my earliest memories sees, or rather hears,
my mother expressing as best she could a sensation that
at the time I took for a real, physical, agony. She felt,
she said (I can picture the scene now: we are in the sitting room of our house, and I have inadvertently done
something to worsen her already fragile condition), as
if her head would explode. Years later, while she was
still alive, I would revise my initial horror at this description, imagining that there was a strict distinction
between mental and bodily pain, that this feeling of being on the point of a real, physical detonation was in fact
a metaphor for a less distinct psychic unease. Much later
again, I would know that she meant nothing so figura-
tive: depression was precisely as palpable a pain as she
had desperately tried to convey to the frightened child in
front of her. But I think I first began to understand the
complete disarray into which her body had drifted over
the years at the moment I knew that her final bout of

187

depression had been brought on by the treatment for her scleroderma. And I think I grasped then, for the first time, the state of confusion in which she had existed for so long: each symptom, each setback adding to her sense of inhabiting a body entirely out of control. As that last mental storm had closed in, she had begun to say that she was going to die soon. I no longer recall whether I thought she really believed this, or whether (because it was not the first time: she had often in the past intimated that she would be 'better off dead') I understood it as a part of her depression. All I remember is my reaction: I simply wanted her to stop saying it; at those moments, I would be overcome by fury, an anger directed not at the circumstance, not at her illness, but at her.

¶ *'a sudden change, and alteration to worse'*
In the years after her diagnosis, my mother's illness seems to me to have ruled our household. This cannot be completely true, but ours seemed a life cut off from those around us. Nabokov's inversion of Tolstoy's famous dictum concerning unhappy families – 'All happy families are more or less dissimilar; all unhappy ones are more or less alike' – has always seemed to me too glib in its paradox. Misfortune, surely, finds unique and inventive forms. An unhappy family feels itself cut off not only from those happy families of legend, but quite painfully aloof too from the miseries of others. A common cliché has it that we can never really know the secrets of a family other than our own. Who knows, asks an ordinary, half-prurient wisdom, what goes on behind closed doors? Less tangible still, though, is the reality of what a family feels like from the inside. It feels, in short, different. I recall distinctly my sense, very early on, that my family was unlike others, and can easily trace that rather shameful sensation. My parents, a little older than the others I saw around me (my father was nearly forty when they married, my mother thirty-three; though I have always, till this minute, when I wrote them for the first time, added a year to their ages), seemed noticeably to have arrived too late on the scene of my childhood. They were a little too austere in their parental strictures, a touch too pious in their religious observance, a decade or two behind the times when compared to the families of my schoolmates. We had no car, took no foreign holidays at a time when that said something about one's outlook and aspirations; my parents dressed as if the sixties had never happened. In all of this, they were far from eccentric, but such details can seem, to a child, to mark a family as distinctly and embarrassingly odd. We

189

were already out of step with the world around us when my mother's disease sent us staggering and sprawling. Although I can pin the change down to no definite date, I know that the beginning of my mother's illness marked an alteration in the way I experienced the chronology of family life, and a shift, therefore, in what and how I am able to remember. Everything I recall is measured according to the advance of her disorder.

In his book *A Fortunate Man*, John Berger has described very precisely the loneliness of the patient who faces a drastic diagnosis:

> As soon as we are ill we fear that our illness is unique. We argue with ourselves and rationalize, but a ghost of the fear remains. And it remains for a very good reason. The illness, as an undefined force, is a potential threat to our very being and we are bound to be highly conscious of the uniqueness of that being. The illness, in other words, shares in our uniqueness.

The difference spreads; it draws those around the suffering person into its obscure circuit, so that they too begin to feel themselves living in another time, as if a whole family had been flung out of the orbit of normality and sent spinning into space. Berger writes:

> The objective coordinates of time and space, which are necessary to fix a presence, are relatively stable. But the subjective experience of time is liable to be so grossly distorted – above all by suffering – that it becomes, both to the sufferer and to any person partially identifying himself with the sufferer, extremely difficult to correlate with time proper.

The family starts to live in accordance with another rhythm, a variable tempo marked by the organizing of hospital appointments, the dull terror of an encroaching diagnosis, the sudden, precipitous speeding up of time occasioned by an emergency in the middle of the night. You live as if time has been splayed and dissected; the rhythm of the calendar – the predictability of future dates hovering in the white space of time yet unlived – feels like it has been drawn into its constituent parts. The future seems both more defined and less knowable. On the one hand: the certainty of appointments, consultations, courses of treatment; on the other: the absolute enigma of an unguessable outcome.

Somewhere between these two incompatible times there unfolds that oxymoronic chronology: the 'progress' of a disease. The brute irony of the term is only the first of the temporal paradoxes in which we are caught. We hurtle towards some definitive end point; we are trapped in our own private, uniform and undeviating time. But other strange chronologies proliferate around us. The world speeds up ('a sudden change, and alteration to worse', writes Donne) but decelerates too, in accordance with the sudden hope of remission or relief, those times when it seems that a conventional gearing of time is possible again, if even for a brief interlude. In the latter case, everything else speeds up: life goes 'on', for a while. What do such dramatic and unpredictable shifts do to our retrospective purchase on events? How can memory begin to reshape a time so creased and stretched? How to recall days, weeks, months and years in which those abstract markers have themselves lost their meaning? I have to stop myself from interpreting everything as a function of the effect of my mother's illness on our lives. But even those periods when it seemed to abate for a while are, from the perspective of the present, marked by what I know is to come.

¶ *Anatomical model*
In 1908, the philosopher Henri Bergson wrote:

> we may speak of the body as an ever-advancing boundary
> between the future and the past, as a pointed end, which
> our past is continually driving forward into our future.
> Whereas my body, taken at a single moment, is but a
> conductor interposed between the objects which influence
> it and those on which it acts, it is, nevertheless, when
> replaced in the flux of time, always situated at the very
> point where my past expires in a deed.

Bergson has in mind the merest sliver of time, which is nonetheless space enough for a body to move, to re-fashion and reorient itself according to the immediate boundaries of past and future. Our bodies, says Bergson, are constantly remaking themselves as they career forward into the unknown, an acceleration that depends on the notion of a vanishing present, an almost invisible instant in which we forget ourselves, as it were, in order to become ourselves again. My body, thus conceived, is nothing but the conduit, as it reaches out into the world, between here and there, then and now (although this 'now' is exactly the problem: where is it?). I forget myself in order to invent myself. I might say that my body as I experience it – in its weariness or exhilaration, its labour or lassitude – is composed of these little vanishing acts: moments of a being which is in fact non-being, only put together in retrospect.

Actually, it is absurd to say that I recognize or truly experience this process. If it were consciously felt, my body would surely cease to function, seized at the most fundamental level by the kind of debilitating self-awareness I glimpse, for example, when I pay too much attention to my own breathing. Bergson's image of a body at one with itself only because it is, in time, unhinged from itself, is perhaps so compelling because I immediately want to extrapolate from it to other, vaster expanses of time. What is it that a body remembers or forgets, considered in its extension into days, months, years? My body seems to repeat, at a level very distant from the microcosm on which Bergson is focussed, the same dialectic of memory and forgetting. I live, according to this wider timeframe, exactly the same oscillation between memory and ignorance. And in my case, the process has a name: hypochondria.

In two cities, a handful of hospitals and several medical practices, there still survive, I suppose, plump folders which attest to my prodigious medical imagination. Together, they would make up a fat autobiographical volume in which the protagonist – a decidedly unreliable narrator – was forever on the point of giving up the ghost, announcing an imminent demise clearly at odds with his talent for sketching new pages and chapters in the chronicle of his decline. This comic narrative of serial delusion – and who knows what profusion of exasperated footnotes a succession of outwardly patient professionals has scribbled in its margins – has now, in my memory, the jerky predictability of a silent movie. The hapless hero speeds, wide-eyed, towards all manner of lethal encounters, only to emerge dishevelled but unharmed, ready for the next absurd interlude. Comedy, says Bergson, happens when a living body acts like a machine. I seem to have spent a good deal of my life submitting my body to the preposterous mechanical repetition of its own imagined end.

I can still feel the overheated waiting rooms in which, time and again, I sat in airless dread of an impending interview, completely convinced that behind a closed door or down a quietly carpeted hallway a doctor was putting aside my notes and setting his or her face into whatever sort of expression it is that one uses to greet a young man on the edge of disaster. I imagined these messengers from my curtailed future to be surprised but professionally intrigued by the extent or swiftness of my disease, somewhat sadly noting the disparity between age and prognosis. I seem to have specialized in contracting the symptoms of a patient three or four times my age. This never occurred to me at the time; my illnesses, I considered, were entirely arbitrary, and therefore perfectly plausible. Why, I reasoned, should fate not afflict me with such ailments? At nineteen, as a boiling summer stretched towards my now unthinkable entry into university, every joint in my body seized up. A stiff, aching knee signalled the start of a general stricture: within days, my spine was a twisted rope of pain, fraying into lesser agonies which eventually unravelled as far as the last joints of my fingers. I spent a fortnight huddled and fearful, eking out the hot days coiled like a superannuated embryo in front of the television, before dragging myself to our family doctor. Who discovered, of course, nothing: except, perhaps, for an unseasonably pallid youth whom he might have done well, had he been less reserved and given a little more thought to family history, to remind that crippling and degenerative disease was rather rare in one of my age. My mind was set on rheumatoid arthritis, though I imagined also certain complications that would ensure a swift decline. But at no point was the warm air of an austere Georgian consulting room disturbed by any reference to my mother's death three years earlier, nor to my father's recent retirement following the sudden onset of suspected heart

195

disease. I left the surgery thinking only of my own unexpectedly spared body, and walked several miles round the city centre, unsure whether the giddiness that kept me moving was elation, embarrassment or the still persisting fear of a pain that had seemed so real only hours before.

A year later, I turned up at the same surgery with exactly the same symptoms. In the middle of my first university exams, the same dull ache traversed my whole body once again, becoming keener and more worrying as it colonized each joint, until eventually I was racked and immobile on my bed. This time, there were blood tests and a more thorough articulation of my unwilling limbs. And again: nothing. I think it was then that I vaguely intuited a correlation between my ailment (which at some level I knew to be fake) and the anniversary of my mother's death. Still, this knowledge did nothing to retard the elaboration of a predictable pattern. Over the next few years, I settled into an almost annual habit. In my early twenties, the onset of summer almost always brought with it a diffuse unease that slowly gathered and refined itself to a sharp point of fear. In solitary hours (my continued studies made sure of too many of these) that fear was refracted into innumerable rays of cold light, illuminating, so I thought, the latest signs of my certain doom. The pattern was always the same: a passing discomfort nursed into darting pain, in turn sublimed in the crucible of a sleepless night into a malign growth or implacable genetic death sentence. Weeks would pass during which I tried to keep my suspicions at bay; I would give vague hints to those around me that I felt unwell, but never come clean about my real fears. It was only when I had reached a point of absolute conviction, certain that my symptoms could denote nothing short of whatever disorder had gripped my imagination this time, that I would make an appointment with a doctor. A few of these fantasized ailments lasted for years. If some of my many crises were easily traced to recent family history (rushed to a cardiac unit, I dragged with me the ghost of my father), others I can only marvel at now, in their baroque inventiveness. Tiny moles grew to deep-rooted melanomic proportions under my gaze; faint rashes flourished, lurid and efflorescent, into lifetimes of disfigurement.

Thinking now of those years of habitual dread, I regret less my misery and fear than I do the sickening waste of time, the hours I spent in dazed and appalled concentration on symptoms which disappeared with even the most cursory examination. I regret those days and weeks spent glumly suspended above my own life, waiting, idiotically, for it to drift far enough away from me to feel that I had entered another, private and almost mythical world. However convinced I might have been, on each occasion, of my impending demise, I was addicted in fact less to melancholy and morbidity than to the ceaselessly replicated moment of resurrection. Emerging from a doctor's surgery with a fresh assurance of my good health, I immediately forgot the horror of only hours before, and could happily return to a life that was not, after all, unpromising. Months, occasionally a whole year (though never more), could go by without interruption, and I found, several times over, that I could talk blithely of my hypochondria as a thing of the past.

Hypochondria, like addiction, is a way of structuring time. It provides a reliable – because supposedly immovable, fatalistic – timetable to those who feel themselves at a loose end between past and future. By a devious logic, the hypochondriac turns his or her feeling of not getting enough from life into an extravagant demand, simply, for more. More life. Nothing of the everyday can match the exhilaration of rebirth that seizes one when the imagined disorder fails to become real. Fixing the date of his good or bad news, the hypochondriac says: from this moment on, my life will change, for better or worse. And the worst, sometimes, seems better than no change at all. But the ruse is compromised, counterproductive. The high doesn't last, and when, inevitably, the ordinariness of things begins to press too hard again, ever more elaborate fears are called for. Over time, your sense of chronology shifts, as if you were really sick and out of phase with the world around you, like a tape recorder looped back on itself, playing and recording at the same time, until eventually all is meaningless noise.

What is it that this noise is designed to drown out? Feeding back on itself, turning a fearfully lived moment into the cacophonous rehearsal of other, identical moments, my mind moved further and further away from the original recording. At the time, the signals were scrambled and undecipherable. I failed to connect them with other, earlier stutterings of my imagination. I had quite forgotten the origins of my fears in a way of experiencing my own body which was, I now acknowledge, a way of reckoning with the agonies of my mother's. It had been a matter, I now recall, of how I lived in my own skin.

¶ Desiccated

I am about twelve years old, and I dream, consistently over a period of several months, this scene. It is morning in my bedroom (the room where I am dreaming). I wake up suddenly, violently shaken (from a dream within a dream?) by some as yet obscure discomfort. As often in nightmares, I both inhabit the dreamed body and see it from a distance: an impossible vantage point, identical to the perspective claimed by those who insist on their out-of-body experiences. What I see from my unlikely position close to the ceiling is this: I wake and immediately, frenziedly, throw back the bedclothes to reveal a body covered from head to toe with livid red marks which are already, in the morning air, hardening to a kind of crust. I stare for a moment, horrified, and my dreaming mind feels the mixture of pain and itch which my dreamt self suffers. The image lasts only for an instant, before the scene shifts to my parents' adjacent bedroom, where I stand weeping tears which sting my raw skin, and saying something I can never hear, no matter how often the dream repeats itself. My parents, indistinct at the other side of the room, remain silent.

The early years of my adolescence were ruled by my skin. Well before the onset of an ordinarily pustular pubescence (*acne vulgaris*: the terminology seems calculated to add to the adolescent's grubby shame), I had begun to live on the surface of a body that gave itself away in frightening and humiliating ways. I must have been about ten when my scalp began to itch, flaking off in a case of dandruff which obstinately resisted all treatments. I itched like the damned. My mother spent hours trying to comb away the evidence. Huge flakes of skin migrated from my scalp to the surface of my hair and from there to my clothes, pillows, to anything I touched.

199

I remember whole afternoons during school holidays vanishing in blizzards of my own skin as I tried to shake away the peelings of my pain (I discovered that there was a state of itchiness indistinguishable from pain). I was adrift in ashy debris, a whirling star chart of my humiliation.

I must have grown used to the feeling that my body was betraying me, because I recall clearly the moment when it stopped being merely an embarrassing nuisance and became an obsession. My mother had recently returned from one of her increasingly regular stays in hospital when, one evening, as she examined my scalp, she wondered aloud whether it might be psoriasis. Suddenly, my suffering had a name, and worse: my mother proceeded to describe (to my father, as if I were not in the room) the psoriatic patients in the ward she had just left. She spoke, I remember, of their condition as if it were worse than her own. I shuddered at her account of a disease I was immediately convinced was about to condemn me to a lifetime of pain and disfigurement. I had no notion that this might be a disorder one could live with, or that my own very mild case was unlikely to blossom into florid and agonizing life all over my body. I thought I was doomed.

Psoriasis became my imagined destiny. Without once voicing my fear to anybody, I began to think of my body as possessed by a hideous secret which was at the same time quite visible to everybody around me. I started to anticipate my body's betrayals; it might give me away at any moment, mark me out as diseased, grotesque, an animated image of decay and barely contained horror. My discomfort, in fact, was in itself manageable: I learned to control the urge, as the itch overcame me like a cloud of tiny biting insects, to scratch till my scalp bled. At times, heat and embarrassment would set up a hideous relay, each feeding the flame of the other until my head might as well have been on fire, such was my distress. I did my best to keep such attacks to myself. But it was more difficult to control the evidence, and I lived in constant fear of having to name the condition that sent an uninterrupted blizzard of dead skin drifting from my raw, red scalp. Haircuts became a trial before which I would have to steel myself for days in case a hairdresser might recoil when faced with the full horror. Of course, my 'condition' was nothing like as appalling as I imagined, and the gap between my extreme reaction and the perception of those around me ought to have been a clue that the origin of my terror lay elsewhere: in a growing, generalized obsession with the frailty of my own bodily integrity. Sometimes, the gap would close. I remember our next-door neighbour, a hairdresser, commenting to my mother that my intractable itch was probably, as she put it, 'psychosomatic'. I remember my mother remarking later that it was odd that I should be afflicted with psoriasis, as sufferers were usually of a 'nervous' disposition. Even at the time (I must have been about twelve), I was amazed that she had failed to notice that I lived in a state of perpetual agitation, and that the source of my fear was precisely my inexplicable itch.

My affliction provided me with an elaborate, and wholly private, personal mythology. I was convinced, for the best part of a decade, that my daily struggle with constant discomfort presaged a lifetime – a brief lifetime – of disease and disfigurement. I suppose it is not unusual for a nervous teenager to imagine not making it to adulthood, but I seem to have taken a sense of my own impending demise to quite outrageous extremes. For a time, I took to hanging around the medical section of our local library, giddy and tearful, amassing grisly evidence of the horrors to come. I foresaw my whole body colonized by livid expanses of weeping and flaking skin. I discovered that the disease might even attack my fingernails, and gave up hours to a vigilant watch over the signs I was sure had already appeared. I found out that at its worst, psoriasis was linked to the onset of a particularly vicious form of arthritis, and began, on the basis of no evidence whatsoever, to calculate how many years of mobility I might have left. At one point, I convinced myself that my perilous prognosis was plain to see, and came to dread even leaving the house. At the slightest glance from a stranger, I fancied that my physical decline was the object of hushed and revolted comment. I fantasized an entire narrative of diagnosis, failed treatment and a miserable future, based on the notion that I would eventually be spotted in the street by a passing dermatologist and swiftly transported to the kind of ward that my mother had once described.

This grim and elaborate fantasy continued for many years. I suppose that I was free of it only in my early twenties, when I had conspicuously failed to succumb to a more concerted and generalized attack, or to acquire any of the ancillary symptoms I was sure were ahead of me. (I had by then anyway substituted other terrors for this one.) I had always imagined that I would be dead by twenty-three: why this specific calculation, I have no idea. In the meantime, I had kept my fears entirely to myself. If they found an outlet, it was in a secret obsession with the life and works of the television playwright Dennis Potter, who famously suffered for most of his adult life from a particularly severe case of psoriatic arthropathy (precisely the prognosis I felt sure awaited me). I had watched *The Singing Detective* – the series in which Potter dramatized his own illness alongside the comically noirish fantasies which his fictional stand-in deploys to take his mind off his ruined body – in horrified fascination. I devoured every published script, every article or interview I could find for references to the writer's illness, feverishly imagining a frail hope for myself in the image of a crippled man making a career for himself out of his circumstance. Potter, I learned, was assured of spending six months of every year completely at the mercy of his disease; the rest, he said, he spent writing. I took to imagining myself similarly constrained, and wondered if I would have the presence of mind to take advantage of what little relief medical science might be able to give me. I must have devoted, if one counts up the remembered hours, whole weeks to such giddy speculations. That I might have been swiftly disabused of my carefully tended terrors by a quick trip to a doctor (it was the one ailment I never took to a doctor) is only the first, comic, irony which they now conjure up for me. (What sort of idiot, I have often wondered since, spends the best part of a decade convinced of his own imminent collapse?) But they seem too to have belatedly taught me something: a lesson about the intimacy of the body, memory and unacknowledged loss.

'Psychosomatic': the word which our neighbour had used so casually to describe my affliction sounded time and again in my mind over the years. I was always half aware that my symptoms were in part invented (this is one of the tricks that hypochondria plays: allowing just enough doubt to let its subject keep a hold on hope, thereby making every real or imagined symptom seem all the more terrifying). The word certainly describes my predicament, but it fails to capture the exact psychological mechanism by which I came to present such a manifest and enigmatic set of signs. An assumption that has passed into common sense tells us that the skin displays on a single plane the obscure and confused depths of unconscious emotion. The skin is a sort of screen on which are projected all the secret and unspeakable fears and desires which we would like to contain (but which we also long to express). According to this way of thinking, all the psychic flow is in one direction: towards the surface, where the emotional slurry we cannot process is poured out on to this pristine surface, scarring it, discolouring it.

The idea that the skin is the visible expression of the unconscious (and not merely, say, the evidence of moral purity or corruption) has its origins in the work of the French psychiatrist Jean-Martin Charcot. From 1862 until his death in 1893, Charcot, as head of the Salpêtrière clinic in Paris, produced a vast photographic record of his 'hysteric' patients and their alarming symptoms. Among the more extraordinary manifestations of their disease (largely performed for the camera at the instruction of Charcot and his colleagues, or painfully induced in accordance with an already documented typology) was the phenomenon of 'dermographia', whereby all manner of telling or mysterious legends were inscribed spontaneously on the flesh of the patients. At least two women are recorded as presenting, on their backs, the word 'Satan'; in one celebrated case, a woman's arm bore the livid inscription 'Urticaria': another name for dermographia. Most, if not all, of these ostensible messages from within were in fact the result of a painful tracing of the words on the skin by Charcot and his staff, or of a crude retouching of the photographic evidence. But such methods could easily (if in bad faith) be excused as bringing out the truth rather than fabricating it, and seem not to have lessened Charcot's faith in the notion that the flesh could speak its pain. Later, his student, Freud, would refine his mentor's overly dramatic scenography of the skin to a more subtle exchange between mind and body (Charcot, said Freud, was not a 'thinker' but an 'artist'). The secrets of the unconscious would no longer be literally written on the body, but would slip out, unnoticed, in a vast array of tiny clues and ciphers: the skin would become a conduit from inside to outside, rather than the parchment on which desire, fear and guilt were carved in legible figures.

In my case, I think, rather, that the skin itself was at issue. I used my skin not to express but to reflect: it was the mirror of the skin with which I could not otherwise reconcile myself: my mother's. The skin, we are told, expresses the self: but it might be equally accurate to say that the self is a function of being in one's skin. Skin (the state of my skin, its prickling or burning, its relative calm, its embarrassing oiliness or dry friability) was what made me, not the other way round. I lived, as it were, at the extremity of my own body: a surface which I thought might betray me without warning, revealing my fearful lack of a comfortable or coherent presence in the world. I was in constant retreat from my skin, and at the same time condemned to keep feeling its sensitivity to the world, to the air, to things: all of which, I imagined, threatened to agitate or injure my skin.

One way to interpret my adventure in my skin might be to say that all of my unspoken fears about my mother's illness had risen to the surface of my own body, there to compose a legible alphabet of expressive fissures and contusions. But over the years I have come to prefer an alternative metaphorical model for the affinity between her disease and my infinitely less serious disorder. In the absence of any way of communicating my turmoil in the face of my mother's illness, it seems to me now that my psoriasis was less an expressive medium than a sort of mirroring: as if, by elaborating my own epidermal map of woe, I could signal across the space between us all that I could not express in words. Perhaps the difference seems excessively subtle; I mean simply this: that although between us no touch seemed possible in those last years of her illness, I had made of my own half-fancied affliction a way of feeling myself closer to her. When she died, I still carried with me, written on my cracked, peeling scalp, a relic of her pain.

My father died on a Monday morning while taking a walk after going to Mass (as, in the last couple of years of his life, he did every day). When, a few hours later, my brothers and I were taken to see his body at the hospital, he was still wearing the clothes in which he had set out that morning. In public, my father's attire hardly varied in all the time I knew him. He made, it is true, some concession to the seasons by varying the weight and thickness of the fabrics he wore, and was even known, especially on holiday, to let himself relax to the extent of wearing a short-sleeved, open-necked shirt. But for the most part he maintained a degree of formality in his dress that was unusual even in a middle-aged civil servant of reasonable seniority and respectable habits. I rarely saw him leave the house without a shirt and tie. Of course, he wore a suit to work, but he never succumbed to the ludicrous fashion (now so generalized as to be invisible) for the 'business suit': his was instead of a more cultured vintage; it denoted respectability and, in his choice of fabrics, a vague intellectualism. Every morning, he would choose from a selection of heavy tweed numbers which he persisted, till the year he died, in having regularly tailor-made at either of the two outfitters (no more current terminology would capture their hushed, archaic air) which seemed to be the only clothes shops he ever frequented. Even his socks were things of sturdy and faintly forbidding fabric: I still possess a single pair, perfectly serviceable if a little too woolly for daily wear. They topped a variety of equally indestructible shoes, each pair polished to such a high sheen that you would think he'd have worn them away over the years, so vigorously did he attack them each Sunday morning. They seemed instead to grow stronger with each frenzied buffeting of brush and cloth, developing a protective layer that was as rigid and impermeable as his overall appearance. But it was mostly his suits that defined him. They varied, over the years, only in the occasional nod to changes in tailoring which could hardly be called fashion: his lapels widened ever so slightly, then contracted as if breathing a sigh of relief once that worrying trend had passed. I suppose that the tailors who made these suits must have prided themselves on ensuring that the customer moved as if he had been born in their garments, but I think my father outdid their expectations: he really did look as though his was a second skin. When I think of my father's physical presence, I think of fabrics: rough tweed, its lighter summer twin, nicely fading corduroy, shirts which might have been starched had my mother actually indulged such old-fashioned excesses (she didn't; he seemed to leach his own starch into them). With such attire came a bearing that never wavered from a poise stuck somewhere between natural elegance and rigid unease. (It is there already in the photograph of my parents crossing O'Connell Bridge: his uprightness might signal confidence or nerves.) It made him look, too, as if he'd arrived from another time entirely: he stands out, even in photographs from his youth, as an emissary from some more dignified, but also hidebound, era.

His elegance didn't save him from the indignity of dying in public: he collapsed in the street, and I wonder now whether the nurses who led me to see his body that summer morning had laid him out as neatly as possible, had re-buttoned his shirt and straightened his tie so that his sons would see the same sedulous attention to detail in his death as they had in the living body that never let down its sartorial guard. Later, after the funeral, the hospital returned to us the clothes in which he had died, bundled in a transparent blue plastic bag. We placed it in a corner of his bedroom, where, as I recall, it remained unopened for years, but not unregarded. I was terrified of opening it, of handling the clothes that had been so close to his death. Instead, I went through the rest of his wardrobe, trying to find something of his that I could wear. I discovered the last suit that he had had made: a lightweight green tweed which he must have worn only a handful of times. I tried on the jacket, but it was too small, as was everything else. And so I found (though I could not have admitted to it at the time) another way of paying belated homage to my father's flawless attire. I started to dress like him, or in as close an approximation as I could muster. I made of my body a sort of secret memorial to my father's lifelong, anachronous attachment to sartorial rigour; I came to believe, I think, that if I could maintain this façade, I would somehow keep at bay the reality of his actual passing. I sported a succession of second-hand tweed jackets and cords, took to wearing (at great cost) leather-soled shoes that required almost monthly repair, ended up unable to venture out without a waistcoat. (I stopped short of the tie: I had at least the presence of mind to realize my scrawny frame couldn't carry off the whole look without a certain comic aspect, which might, of course, have been present anyway.) And when I began to suspect my motive for this neurotic reliance on always looking the same, I had at least the consolation that its origin passed largely unnoticed: I could easily be dismissed as a rather tediously fastidious youth. In truth, I had come to resemble, by an affinity which is less morbid than it first appears, my father's corpse: an image carefully composed to mask a mournful truth.

Years later, I have this dream. I am in our family's house, standing in the hall, and I know (though they're not yet visible) that my brothers and my father are there too. Everything is more or less as it had been, except for one detail that immediately strikes me as odd: it is night, and every light in the house is on. The doors leading off the hall are closed, and I move towards the staircase unseen. As I climb the stairs, I listen for my father's presence: if he discovers that the whole house is illuminated, he will, I imagine, immediately start turning lights off, closing doors, reminding me that he is paying for my comfort (the house is warm, too: even here on the landing, everything seems bathed in an uncharacteristic glow). But I'm not unduly worried: the house is quiet and I suppose that my father is downstairs in the sitting room, in his usual armchair, reading. On the landing, I look to my left and notice that my parents' bedroom door is slightly ajar: I can see that there, too, the light is on. I open the door a little further and slip into the empty room, where again nothing has changed from the time I knew it. That is, it looks like an impossible version of itself: all my parents' belongings are there, as if every stage in the room's history had somehow come to inhabit the same moment. Just inside the door, several untidy stacks of books totter alongside the wall, the last few piled a little higher in the corner between the right-hand wall and the large, white, built-in wardrobe in front of me. One of its doors is open: inside, I can make out the dull green of my father's last suit. The bed to my left looks freshly made: on the left, a single pillow for my father; on the right, two or three piled up where my mother slept with her head raised (a sign of her illness, I now realize: her restricted airways demanded it). On either side of the bed, all the usual paraphernalia are intact: yet more stacks of books on the left, and in the narrow space in front of them, a tiny radio with a single earpiece. The table on the right holds, as expected, a neater collection of my mother's books: on top, her Bible. Still alert for a sound downstairs, I round the end of the bed to come into the other side of the room, where my parents' dressing table stands as before by the window. Everything that ought to be there is apparently in its proper place: my father's pipes, his ashtray and tattered brown wallet, my mother's jewellery, her black plastic hairbrush (between its white bristles, a net of jet-black hair). But something is subtly different: the wood of the dressing table seems to glow, reflecting a light that I do not remember as ever having been so bright in this room.

I sit down on the bed, facing the dressing table, and look straight ahead into its central mirror (from here, I think, I can see anybody who comes into the room behind me). Below the mirror are two deep drawers whose contents I remember clearly. The bottom one is my father's: in there, I know, are numerous discarded ties, old sweaters knitted by my mother, a few frayed shirts and a couple of bottles of unused aftershave. I grab the brass handles of the top drawer and slide it open slowly, recalling neat piles of carefully ironed clothes belonging to my mother. They are not there; instead, the drawer seems to have been tightly packed with white bedsheets, slightly yellowed with age. My dreaming mind briefly registers this slight change, but the detail is not enough to jolt me out of the bright reality of the room. I slip a hand down either side of the fabric, where there is just enough room for me to reach along the rough interior to the bottom of the drawer and grasp its contents, which now reveal themselves to compose a tightly rolled or folded package. The whole thing comes out easily, sagging in the middle as I notice that it is heavier than it first appeared, as if it were made of more than elderly cotton. I lift the soft parcel on to the bed, and as I do so I realize that it is warm. In fact, its heat is already spreading on to the floral quilt on which I'm sitting, and the unaccustomed warmth of the whole house is now beginning to make sense: it seems to emanate from the pale bundle in front of me. I start to unwrap the first layer of fabric: a vast sheet which unravels slowly till I can cast it aside on the bed. Inside, a thicker material of the same dingy white encloses three or four more lozenges, each one rolled, then tucked tightly into itself at both ends. Now that they are exposed, I can see that there is something inside: each one bulges in various directions, and as I reach out to touch the first I can feel that whatever is hidden in these strange rolls of fabric, it is rigid. I pull on the ends of the first roll and begin to unwrap it. When I have unfolded it to its full extent across the bed and uncovered the hard mass at its centre, I am looking down at a small pile of bones.

The sight is, strangely, unshocking. Only later would I imagine (mistakenly, I now believe) that this dream dramatized the unthinkable revelation of and reckoning with some dark, repressed horror; at the time, the whole scene was overlain by a bright and fearless calm. I pick up the largest (pure white in contrast to the now murkier background) and feel its heat for a moment before putting it back. At that moment, my two brothers appear in the room beside me; I must have missed their footsteps on the landing outside. They stand by the bed, looking first at me, then at my bizarre discovery, but they say nothing, and I take this as a signal to carry on. But as I reach for the second parcel, my father is suddenly at the door, and the three of us turn towards him silently as if to ask his permission to reveal the next cache of what I know will be more relics from the same luminous ossuary.

On awaking, I could no longer recall precisely what my father said, only this certainty: that he had given us to understand that it was not yet time to expose the remaining contents of the drawer. I felt, I think, that this was less a warning than a simple statement about the proper timing of such a revelation: my father wasn't angry, just concerned that I should not rush a discovery which would come in time. And so, carefully, and under the calm gaze of my father and brothers, I wrapped those few bones back in their protective fabric and placed them in the drawer of the dressing table, pushing it closed again as a last gentle gush of warm air escaped the folds.

PLACES

'Memory, like the mind and time, is unimaginable
without physical dimensions; to imagine it as a physical
space is to make it into a landscape in which its contents
are located, and what has location can be approached.'
— Rebecca Solnit, *Wanderlust: A History of Walking*

'Space is a doubt: I have constantly to mark it, to
designate it. It's never mine, never given to me, I have
to conquer it. ... Space melts like sand running through
one's fingers. Time bears it away and leaves
me only shapeless shreds.'
— Georges Perec, *Species of Spaces*

¶ *Labyrinth*

It is possible to imagine the whole story of one's child-hood in the form of a list of places occupied: the relative safety of the house, the deadening or fraught space of the classroom, the giddy flux of the first city street on which one became lost. There was a period in my life when I had lost all sense of how these and other places might co-here to form a landscape in which I felt that I belonged. In truth, I had cultivated this sense of placelessness. I did my best to avoid passing through the area where I grew up, turned my head when a bus from one side of the city to another came too close to one of the hospi-tals in which my mother had been a patient (or worse, the hospital where she died), and neglected to visit my parents' grave. I thought I could map the city on a new scale, abstracted from the past and dotted with forget-ful blanks. But I was forever being reminded of those parts of the picture I had hoped to erase. They seeped through the overpainted surface of my memory. Streets all seemed to lead to the same district. Without a link to the place where I grew up, other, fleeting memories of the city started to awaken, and I found that certain city-centre shops – places I'd been to with my mother twenty years earlier – were horribly oppressive. My habit of avoidance had seemed to accelerate to catch up with me, so that even more recent memories quickly be-came intolerable to me. Eventually, what had started as a strategy for avoiding the most haunted places in the city began to spread to the whole territory, so that in time I could hardly bear to be there at all. I recall a visit some years ago, having been away for a couple of years, when I found myself quite suddenly unable to walk the streets of Dublin without being overcome by a sense that every place was haunted by my previous life there. I hurried back to my new home convinced that I could never set foot in the city again.

What we persist in calling time is in fact only the evidence of movement in space, inscribed in the world around us in so many useful, exhilarating ways: the motion of a clock's hands, the exuberance or languor of the seasons, the infinitesimal or suddenly accelerated erosion of a face or body. At times, this insight seems to impress itself upon us with an unexpectedly personal weight of meaning, an import which, at moments of uncertainty or regret, we might be tempted to mistake for something cosmically or spiritually significant: a sense that our own fleeting consciousness is the sole medium in which disparate moments of time and points in space might be said to come together to form a design of sorts. At such junctures, we can be tempted to picture ourselves in heroic solitude amongst the whirling garbage of space and time, or, alternatively, attuned to some higher frequency: the touch of a divinity which brings all things into harmonious consort. But I can credit neither the notion that memory orbits a Romantically inclined monad of consciousness, nor that this singular (and perhaps vacant) point is plenished by any pretence at spiritual fulfilment. I count myself a materialist when it comes to memory: that is to say, I take some comfort from the thought that I am the product, thrust into the foreground, of a haphazard spatial backdrop, not its centre, still less its master.

Yet there is the seduction of imagining oneself at the centre of something, of making the places to which memory adheres circulate according to some system. I am still attracted, for example, many years after my first reading, by a passage in Walter Benjamin's *A Berlin Chronicle*, which seems to suggest precisely a method for imagining the past without succumbing to the idealist fantasy that it exists to guarantee one's own central presence:

> Now on the afternoon in question I was sitting inside the Café des Deux Magots at St-Germain-des-Prés, where I was waiting – I forget for whom. Suddenly, and with compelling force, I was struck by the idea of drawing a diagram of my life, and knew at the same moment exactly how it was to be done. With a very simple question I interrogated my past life, and the answers were inscribed, as if of their own accord, on a sheet of paper I had with me. A year or two later, when I lost this sheet, I was inconsolable. I have never since been able to restore it as it arose before me then, resembling a series of family trees. Now, however, reconstructing its outline in thought without directly reproducing it, I should, rather, speak of a labyrinth.

At the centre of this maze of memory, writes Benjamin, is perhaps 'ego or fate'; but this is not what interests him. Rather, he is intrigued by the passages that lead to this too-mystical centre: 'so many primal relationships' with individuals, these are what compose the picture of his life. When I first read this passage, I too was sitting in a café, waiting: the coincidence afforded me a small thrill of self-aggrandizement, and the fragment of a cigarette packet which still marks the page in question reminds me that my friends' arrival startled me out of a reverie that immediately seemed somewhat pretentious. For a moment, I had wondered what a graphic representation of my own life might look like, and concluded that I would be incapable of filling in the inner circles of my memorial labyrinth. How, I thought, could I possibly overcome my reticence to speak of, or even properly reflect on, the still, to my mind, very recent cataclysms that had befallen my family? The last thing I wished to consider with any kind of clarity was exactly the nature of those 'primal relationships'. And anyway, I thought, what possible use could such an acknowledgement of the recent past really have? For a moment, however, before I closed the book, I had a picture before me of another kind of cartography, a map that would better capture my very distance from those events. The diagram, I thought, would be almost uninhabited: the true picture would not record my relationships with individuals, but with the places that still pressed on my imagination.

¶ *A seizure of the heart*

In George Eliot's *Middlemarch*, the novelist has her ardent heroine Dorothea – who has recently, filled with intellectual and spiritual idealism, married the arid scholar Casaubon – react with a morbid horror to the lavish surroundings of her Roman honeymoon. While her husband abandons her for his historical research, Dorothea is left to wander, uncomprehending, among the worrying splendours of classical and ecclesiastical Rome. Dorothea, 'fed on meagre protestant histories and an art chiefly of the hand-screen sort', is unprepared for the brooding intricacies of Catholic iconography:

> Forms both pale and glowing took possession of her young sense, and fixed themselves in her memory even when she was not thinking of them, preparing strange associations which remained through her after-years. Our moods are apt to bring with them images which succeed each other like the magic-lantern pictures of a doze; and in certain states of dull forlornness Dorothea all her life continued to see the vastness of St Peter's, the huge bronze canopy, the excited intention in the attitudes and garments of the prophets and evangelists in the mosaics above, and the red drapery which was being hung for Christmas spreading itself everywhere like a disease of the retina.

The denominational specifics of this passage are not what interest me, nor yet the echoes it might attract of my own Catholic childhood. What accosts me first here instead is Eliot's insistence on the way in which the interior of the church persists in Dorothea's imagination. Its oppressiveness is only partly a matter of theology; it arises mostly, I surmise from my own recollections, from a particular conjunction of architecture and atmosphere,

220

of light and stone. Because the first place I wish to recall here is a church: a building which, in its monstrous presence in my childhood and its harrying significance in later years, has never ceased to come back to me in the form of certain ill-lit but persistent images.

As a child, I knew little of the history of the church; I have only just discovered, courtesy of a website tended by a devoted parishioner, the details of its early years. Mount Argus church, situated to the west of what was then the village of Harold's Cross, was completed in 1878, built to replace an earlier structure erected twenty-two years earlier by the Passionist order. The Passionists (or, to give them their full title, The Congregation of Discalced Clerks of the Most Holy Cross and Passion of Our Lord Jesus Christ) had purchased the land surrounding a modest manor house in 1856, and had by the end of the year built their first church and already, by all accounts, attracted a large congregation. Worshippers were drawn, it seems, by the reputation (but also by the tireless efforts) of the first rector, Fr Paul Mary Packenham. The young priest, a nephew of the Duke of Wellington, had only recently completed a notable military career and scandalized his family and social circle by first converting to Catholicism, then entering the priesthood and finally (to the extreme consternation of friends and family) leaving England for his native Dublin to found the community at Mount Argus. Within a year of the consecration of his church, Packenham was dead, having suffered some months earlier a 'seizure of the heart'. But he had already set in motion a building scheme that would see the completion in 1863 of a large monastery adjoining the church, and the plans for a much larger church to replace the one now dwarfed by the imposing grey stone of

221

a building which one contemporary account considered 'the noblest religious house erected in these countries since the so-called "reformation"'. The new church was designed to accommodate a congregation of six hundred, seated below vast arches and flanked by huge columns of mottled brown marble. Later, in 1924, one could look up from one's pew and see a series of enormous paintings, vertiginously angled towards the kneeling worshippers below, which depicted such scenes as the Coronation of Our Lady, Christ and the Apostles or the order's Italian founder, St Paul of the Cross.

Those paintings were still there when I was a child, now considerably blackened and indistinct. Although I knew that a second row of canvases arrayed below showed the Stations of the Cross, I could never penetrate the gloom above them to work out what these dark rectangles were supposed to represent. The obscuring patina they had acquired over the decades was always linked in my mind to the enormous badges worn by the Passionists themselves: fat black hearts that hung from their robes as they passed by my seat or disappeared into a confessional towards which I would shortly have to make my way, praying as much for my terror to abate as for any forgiveness I might find there. When I recall the inside of the church, I remember first of all its shadows, and the way a black shape always seemed to be moving just beyond my field of vision, emerging from a doorway leading from the monastery (I would always try to catch a glimpse of that mysterious interior, but never saw more than a sliver of pale wall and dark tiled floor), or busying itself about a huge brass rack of candles in a recess off the main body of the church. During a Mass, as all eyes were fixed on the brightly lit altar or sunk towards the floor in an attitude I found utterly unsettling (I could never replicate that peculiar prostration: I think I was petrified of the visions that might accost me if I closed my eyes and bowed my head like all the muttering wraiths around me), I felt these hollows lurking behind me. There, numerous statues hovered, agitated by the candlelight as if subject to some pious, ecstatic tremor, or palsied by their legendary, sinful pasts. Some looked more benign than others. To enter the church, you had to come face to face with a fairly faded and chipped St Anthony: an unthreatening figure whose plaster might have been cracked and bruised by all those endless forays for lost or stolen objects to which he was daily condemned. (Of all the saints, and their various and sometimes improbable métiers, his has always seemed to me the most tragic: an unthinkable eternity spent scrabbling about for the paltry detritus of mortal lives.) Once inside, you could glimpse at least one pallid Virgin in the gloom, a placid mass of white and blue above the yellow candlelight. I hoped, always, to advance quickly from this part of the church towards the light at the other, altared, end: thus to avoid even a glance to the right, at the most thrillingly awful spot in the whole building. Here, in a cavernous pendule of the church proper, was a small chapel which I remember as being perpetually dark. It seemed to be frequented by the most pious, but also the most hopeless, worshippers: individuals who would fling themselves on to their knees at its thick brass balustrade and remain there indefinitely, mumbling indecipherable imprecations to the darkness. A still more distressing sight was to be found to their left, high on the wall above me on the rare occasions when my mother led my brothers and me into this dank offshoot of the main space of the church. Here, a small patch of glass enclosed a tiny remnant of fabric which a legend below informed me had touched the dead body of a saint whose name I have now quite forgotten. The narrative that attached to this grisly relic was beside the point: what terrified me was the object itself, a dull grey morsel of mortality which seemed, encased in its vitreous circle, like a single, baleful eye, looking down on me accusingly. I dreaded its implacable gaze; on at least one occasion I was petrified by my mother's encouraging me to reach out and touch it.

That grim corner was linked in my mind to a matching, but daylit, spot at the other end of the church, where the body of a long-dead Passionist lay beneath a vast, whitish marble tomb. This was the grave and the shrine of Father Charles Houben, a Dutch-born priest who had come to Mount Argus in 1857. Father Charles, it was said during his lifetime, had the power to heal diseases of both mind and body; he preached to huge crowds outside the church, inviting them to reflect on the Passion to which his order was devoted. It seems that his miraculous potency had only increased in the years since his death in 1893, and by the time I was brought to kneel at his grave he was a candidate for canonization. Beside the shrine, his story was recounted in livid red letters: his legendary piety, his apparently numerous cures and his fortitude, towards the end of his life, in bearing the pain of an ulcerated leg caused by a carriage accident. It might well have been this last anecdote that I latched on to as I turned to look at an engraving that showed Charles Houben preaching to a vast throng on the steps outside. Each time we knelt before this otherwise untroubling shrine, I was secretly appalled to note that the black-robed figure at the centre of the picture appeared to be holding, in a hand raised high above the crowd, a bone. I could never work out what macabre rite was being enacted here, though I fully understood that the bone must be human. I never asked my parents about this image (it was mostly with my mother that I would have knelt there), but left the shrine, always, with a mixture of relief and dread.

Quite apart from its habitually dismal atmosphere and lurking horrors, the church was the scene of a series of unsettling episodes and one singular and alarming event. A strict Freudian (and therefore a crude Freudian, unlike Freud himself) might identify them as 'screen memories': those remembered events which act to occlude the real matter of memory, whose outlines the analyst draws out from behind the mask of these manifest disguises. The first is itself a kind of occlusion. I must have been about ten years old when it first happened: a series of fainting episodes which arrived quite punctually halfway through the Sunday Mass we always attended (eleven o'clock: the 'Family Mass'). I remember that, on each occasion, it started with a gradual and unnerving awareness of the space around me. The vastness of the church seemed to swell and contract around me, the amplified voice of the priest oscillating in time with this movement, as if the whole building were breathing heavily. I became uncomfortably aware of the borders of my field of vision: the nameless paintings seemed to crowd at its edges until I realized that it was not their dark shapes that were intruding towards the centre, but a more amorphous gloom, pressing towards a brightness somewhere in the vicinity of the altar on which I tried to focus.

The first time it happened, I must have leapt back from my kneeling position before the shadow closed around the figure of the priest who now seemed to be speaking from a distant and tiny vantage far in the depths of space, because I remember clearly that as I was led out of the church (I can no longer say whether it was my father or mother who took me home), I felt sure that I had just been on the point of death. An unlikely outcome, of course, but a certainty that seized me in the subsequent months during which the same terrifying plunge towards the edge of consciousness became an inevitable part of my family's weekly worship. Perhaps it says something about my parents' odd reticence to address my increasingly nervous disposition at that time that I became so convinced of the proximity of my own demise. More likely, it was one of those secret fears that a child tends as if it were the guarantee of his own singularity: an image of something just below the surface of family life which might at any moment undo its texture of habit and routine. It seems clear to me now that I had turned my vague comprehension of my mother's illness into my own minor drama of physical failure, and that my fear was somehow bound up with this place: the church which seemed already to promise a deathly future.

During the school holidays, my mother was in the habit
of taking my brothers and me to the church on a summer afternoon: a regular visit I never questioned at the
time but which I now recognize as part of her increasing recourse to prayer in the face of her failing physical
condition. On those bright afternoons, the building
seemed especially oppressive, its acres of cold marble lit
by numerous tiny candles to which we would add a few:
always my mother's last gesture before leaving. Often,
the dolefulness of these visits was given an extra layer
of tedium by the ritual of confession. I can picture, on
the day in question, the immediate sequel to one such
ordeal: I am seated beside my mother, towards the front
of the church. We have just emerged from confession
and I am dutifully rehearsing my allotted penance,
though no longer, I suspect, entirely crediting the idea
I had always had of the purifying effect of absolution.
I have ceased to imagine that somewhere to the right of
my heart is a pure white sphere, just now washed clean
of the black sinful stains that had accrued over weeks: it
is my immortal soul. Seated in the church, I am vaguely aware of the presence, in the pew in front of us, of
a familiar figure: a shabbily dressed man whom I have
often seen in the same place, and who I understand to
be at least eccentric, possibly 'simple', at worst mad. As
always, he sits quietly, attending to a small pile of school
exercise books on the seat beside him. He opens each
book in turn, flicks through the pages, reads for a moment, and replaces it in the pile as he takes up another.
He is almost part of the furniture of the church: a figure
I have grown used to, as I'm used to the fading green
fabric of the kneeler at my feet or the brass plaque above
it which records the name of the donor who paid for this

particular pew. I try to keep my eyes on its polished surface, but I am aware of a movement to the right of it: the copybook man is on his feet and moving towards the altar. He reaches the thick gilt gate at the centre of a low marble balustrade which separates the altar from a wide central aisle. He opens the gate and crosses the dark red carpet to reach a high pulpit to the left; at the top of its steps he places his collection of tattered copybooks on the lectern, looks up and begins to speak. I have no idea what he is saying; the microphone in front of him is switched off. I am now completely terrified, though I notice that the people around me – my mother, my brothers and the usual scattering of elderly churchgoers – seem only mildly perplexed, even amused, by this unintelligible sermon. I can't make my mother understand that I am utterly unnerved by the figure before me, who seems already to have thought better of his homiletic adventure and is even now gathering his books together and edging away from the pulpit. Eventually, my mother seems to notice my agitation, and we leave hurriedly; as we cross the car park and descend the steep hill to the gates of the church grounds, she tries to convince me that there is nothing to be afraid of, that he is only unwell, a 'poor soul'. And although I understand that my reaction was unnecessary, indeed unfair to an unfortunate individual who posed no threat, I am haunted by his image for days, more unsettled than I will ever let on, as if I had witnessed some sudden unveiling of the everyday, its revelation as a sham; as if I'd glimpsed the possibility that anybody, myself included, might, without warning, do the same.

What I remember of this place, then, is in fact my urge, on these occasions, to flee it. It was not so much a solid place as a void into which I used to feel I might fall: I would gaze, in distracted moments, at its upper reaches, and wonder what it would be like to drift towards the distant ceiling and hang there, looking down on the congregation below. And yet it was also the site of a very palpable set of sensations, the locus of a form of boredom and lethargy which I do not think I've felt anywhere else. Perhaps it is only as children that we experience a species of tedium that verges on physical pain. This boredom has to do with the intolerable weight of things, their pointless perdurance and arbitrary condensation into, for example, the vastness of the church's empty upper reaches, less uplifting than insufferably weighty. It is apparently one of the inescapable duties of parenthood to inform a child of the sinfulness of boredom (a favoured theme of my father's: it is only now that I wonder whether there was an ironic inflection to his resort to the cliché that only the boring are bored). But boredom, surely, teaches us something beyond mere stamina; it informs us of the dumb endurance of things despite all efforts to make them speak and move according to a system (the combination of architecture and theology, say). And if the church taught me, as it seems now to have done, that the spiritual lesson I was supposed to learn there was nothing but a gloss over fear, shame and suffering, it must also have inculcated in me a sense that at the heart of all that was just the meaningless persistence of matter. I know this much: never have I been so extravagantly, so painfully, so metaphysically bored as in the hours I spent surrounded by its iconography. The philosopher Leibniz once wrote that 'marble has ideas, however confused', and it strikes me now that the substance of that building had a kind of miserable eloquence, that in the yellowed veins of its stones was a message about the physical world itself. The marble, I think, may have got into my blood.

¶ Removal

By the time my mother died in the summer of 1985, I had grown to truly loathe this place. In my mind, for a moment, it is still always Gothic, before I remind myself that its late-Victorian pretensions are in fact to a more sturdy and Romanesque design. My hatred of its obscenely mottled marble columns and monstrous arches increased in proportion with the frequency of my mother's visits. The church functioned already, it seems, to separate us from our immediate locale, and to partake of a different sense of place from that encouraged, for example, by the local school I attended till I was ten years old, and the church to which it was affiliated. Mount Argus church was in fact in an adjacent parish to ours, and we went there, rather than the more modest, airy and modern (mid-twentieth-century) church of our parish, a few hundred yards in the opposite direction, largely because it had been for decades the church to which my father's family had gone. (It was, and is perhaps still, traditionally the church of the city's police force, since the days of my grandfather's joining what was then the Dublin Metropolitan Police.) I recall an enraged priest from our parish church actually accosting and berating my mother from the pavement outside our house, bellowing intemperately (probably drunkenly, I now realize) that his church wasn't 'good enough' for her. I think I can plausibly date my definitive falling away from faith to that afternoon, and the sight of this florid-faced, proprietorial cretin, comically talking up his own particular franchise on the divine.

I understood, however, that there was something unusual about our church. It was a sort of family secret, a habit that set us apart. It seemed somehow more rooted in a vaguely defined ecclesiastical history than any of the others (and there were many) we visited over the years. I think I may even, when very young, have got it into my head that God lived in our church: the others were just temporary residences hastily pulled together out of second-rate materials, prim decor and decidedly less supernaturally charged paraphernalia. I marvelled at the apparent informality (I didn't know it was just another sort of stricture) of country churches where women and children sat at the front while their menfolk, having loitered at length outside, smoking and talking in low voices, shuffled in to lurk, standing, at the back, as if the whole affair were no more deserving of their devout attention than a speech by some local dignitary or a show of less than prime livestock. Elsewhere, the crucifixes were less gruesome than I was used to, the altars seemed shrunken and hardly fit to house the central mystery of the Mass, the confessionals lacked the requisite embellishments that towered above me, promising elaborate punishment, and the statuary was too cheerful by far to capture properly the solemn benediction of a saint whose sufferings, at our church, would have been startlingly emblematized. Still, despite the deity's fleeting presence in these other churches, there was a kind of relief in escaping the gorgeous horror of 'our' church for less imaginatively demanding spaces, like the parish church we visited three Sundays a year during our summer holidays in Kerry.

We never made it to that church in the summer of 1985. Instead, we arrived at Mount Argus on the evening before my mother's funeral for what is called, again according to a terminology which is both literal and euphemistic, 'the removal'. I remember nothing of it; not the tall black gates of the church grounds, nor the towering façade of the building itself, with its huge stone angel perched between two massive spires. In my memory, the angel is golden, and though I know this to be an invention of my later recollection of a figure that could be seen plainly several streets away from the church, it is still gilt and shining as I try to picture that evening. I don't recall the scene as we entered the church, the backs of the mourners gathered tightly at the front, nor the coffin which must have been inches away from us in the central aisle, nor the service itself, nor the walk back out of the church to the waiting car. The following morning is clearer in my mind: I remember hoping my legs would not buckle under me as I walked from our seat at the front of the church to the altar to read a prayer; I remember the endless parade of mourners who shook my hand and that some of them (those I didn't know) murmured that they were sorry for my trouble (I recall too how I dreaded this phrase five years later, standing in the same place); I remember the long procession towards a square of daylight at the rear of the church, and how as we passed the place where my family sat every Sunday morning I had an odd sense that we were still there, that if I could just focus on the right spot in the crowd I would catch sight of my childhood self, starting to feel queasy and light-headed in the midst of the throng.

Another summer in the same church: the same faces passed in front of me; I stood on the same altar and looked down at the same two bodies of dark figures, either side of my father's coffin. This time, I was to deliver one of the two readings, and not only did my voice only waver once, but later I was told that I had displayed an impressive calm and even managed to modulate my delivery sufficiently not to sound as if I were reading a passage I had rehearsed several times in my head the night before. I understood that my self-possession was a function of my distance from the whole spectacle. I think, in fact, that I had given up any sense that all of this was happening to me: rather, the church had somehow taken over and I was simply submitting myself to its demands, to the sinister urges concealed in its stony soul. I remember that I hated it more than ever that second morning, and couldn't wait to get out, away from the rituals that meant nothing, the hideous familiarity of every inch of the stone and wood (now garishly renewed; the church had closed and been refurbished some weeks after my mother's funeral), the vilely ornamented confessionals and pathetic, placarded attempts at quickening the deathliness of the space with invitations to less life-sapping formulations of the Mass. I felt too that the funeral had exposed our ancient family secret: our affinity with this monstrous architecture, this unbearable weight of solid silence and droning piety, these poisonous clouds of incense and candle smoke.

¶ *Terre de Marie*
Some time ago, when this present book had yet to come into focus in my mind, and before I had properly acknowledged that a reflection on memory might also be a reflection on *my* memory, I spent an afternoon in the junk shops of a small coastal town near my home. Amongst the debris of numerous nameless lives, I discovered – lost, perhaps, for decades – at the back of one such establishment, a curious object. It is a small white folder, considerably tattered, on which is printed, in fading red letters, these words: 'Véronèse présente: Lourdes, Terre de Marie. 32 Diapos sur film Kodak, avec texte Français, English, Italiano, Deutsch'. A flimsy booklet is attached to the inside of the front cover, and its thin pages describe, in thirty-two numbered paragraphs, the contents: a series of tiny slides slotted into a crackling plastic grid, which I unfolded with a quite unexpected, and still unfathomable, sense of familiarity. The slides, as the title suggests, depict, in colours that are still lucidly those of photographs which appear to have been taken in the 1960s, a variety of views of the French town and its famous shrine.

I have never been to Lourdes; the place exists for me only in my imagination – as it does, I suspect, for even the most devoutly educated of my generation – as a distant, if not somewhat disturbing, anachronism. There was a time, of course, when this place – its name traditionally mispronounced: one could trace, I imagine, the date of its disappearance from collective fantasy according to the silencing of the final 's' which generations of Irish voices gave it – seemed to me to be a distant outpost of Ireland itself: an offshore appendage of the world I knew as a child. It was, for example, for many years the only foreign place to which I could be sure members of my family had actually been. I knew little then of its history, beyond the familiar and periodically rehearsed tale of Bernadette Soubirous, who, in 1858, was said to have witnessed, over a period of two weeks, the apparition of the Virgin Mary. I had heard nothing, for example, of the controversies which attended its early celebrity: the struggles which unfolded, in the last decades of the nineteenth century, over both the original episode and its historical legacy: the fame of Lourdes as a place of healing and pilgrimage.

I wonder now precisely what brought my mother to Lourdes. The question is in part a foolish one, and its answer painfully clear: she wanted to be cured. But I cannot, despite my recollection of her periodic trips there, quite imagine how she must have felt as she set out on her journey, nor whether that hope of relief from her symptoms was for her a real possibility or the unthinkable end point of a continuum that must have included the more modest aspiration to spiritual consolation. I remember that she travelled on at least one occasion with one of her sisters, and that later the prayer group she attended weekly at our local church went en masse. And I recall that on those occasions I had an image in my mind of what a 'cure' meant, drawn from a story which is itself obscure in my memory: of a woman healed (of what illness I never knew) at one of the huge prayer meetings my mother attended every few months. The single detail I recall of that event is this: that the woman's body was overcome at the moment of her apparent cure by an extraordinary heat. I remember that my father dismissed this supposed miracle (and the bout of glossolalia which, my mother reported, accompanied it) with a word I only vaguely understood ('hysteria') but which I would later come to resent even as my own scepticism grew. And so I must surmise that what my mother hoped for was something more than spiritual consolation or the comfort of a collective act of pilgrimage. She must, I think, actually have imagined a real physical transformation. The historical accounts of those ostensibly cured at Lourdes treat dramatically of this instant of transfiguration, recounted always as a kind of convulsion, struggle, and final expulsion by the pilgrim's body of his or her disease. Even in the viciously sceptical account of Emile Zola, whose novel *Lourdes*, in 1894, was variously received as either a scandalous slander or a timely revelation of the miracle factory that the shrine had become, it is hard not to be moved by the fictional testimony of one Marie de Guersaint, a character who claims to have been healed at the moment the Eucharist, in procession, passed by her:

"It was my legs the Blessed Virgin freed first ... I could feel clear as anything the irons that bound them sliding over my skin, like broken chains. ... Then the weight that was always stifling, here, in my left side, rose up my body. ... But it went right past my throat, I had it in my mouth and I spat it out as hard as I could. ... That was it, my illness was gone – flown away."

Was this the sort of seizure my mother, her deepest hopes encouraged by the narratives bequeathed by previous visitors to this place, had imagined? By the time she went there, such vivid imagery (nineteenth-century cures are typically described in these physical terms: the miracle is often symbolically a sort of childbirth) was less common, and the distinction between the sick and the healthy had even begun to be elided in favour of a less dramatic emphasis on spiritual community.

Still, that original hope, the possibility of a sudden cure, must have been alive beneath my mother's devotion to the public ritual of pilgrimage. On her return, I recall, she sometimes spoke about her fellow pilgrims. I pictured them arrayed in wheelchairs, in beds, attended by spouses and nurses, awaiting their immersion in the waters. I always imagined Lourdes as a tiny village, like the village of my mother's own childhood. I am quite certain that in the years during which my mother travelled to Lourdes, I never once saw a photograph of the town, or heard her describe the place itself, its landscape, the grotto itself or the basilica which I now know to have been the place of her hopeful worship. The Lourdes that loomed in my mind was a hamlet as crudely built as the story of its original apparitions suggested.

I had imagined Lourdes on an intimate scale, and the slides which lie before me now reveal, as I raise each one to the light, portions of that miniature landscape into which I had inserted my mother's ailing body. For example, in a photograph captioned simply 'Piscines', two assistants are lowering an old man into the water. The space in which his immersion takes place is surprisingly austere: bordered by tiled walls to which are attached metal bannisters which the two attendants grip as they lower their charge into a central stone-lined pool. The scene has the look, to my unbelieving eye, of an interment, and the ritual seems quite unaltered from that depicted in an engraving I have seen from 1880, in which all that piety adds to the spectacle is a priest's hand raised in blessing and an unlikely shaft of divine light descending from the ceiling to illuminate the face of the pilgrim (a face still sufficiently obscure that its expression might as easily denote bodily discomfort as spiritual ecstasy). For the most part, in these photographs, the pilgrims appear in crowds of stretchers and wheel-chairs, their anonymous backs to the camera, 'assisting' (as the French has it) at several sorts of worship. They are blessed in harsh sunlight in front of the Parvis du Rosaire, and circle the brightly lit concelebrants in the Basilique St Pie X. One imagines them gazing up at the numerous statues depicted here: a towering Virgin, an ecstatic Bernadette, a monstrous Calvary. The place I had imagined as a meekly devout enclave is in fact a virtual metropolis, dedicated, in its open spaces and cavernous interiors, to a kind of miraculous industry. With its wide avenues, and its administrative machinery devoted to moving masses of people from one place of worship to another, Lourdes, in fact, looks remarkably of a piece with the secular modernity to which it was os-tensibly opposed in the nineteenth century.

None of those panoramic views or busy interiors held as much fascination, however, as did a singular-ly detailed photograph which I found among them. It shows, according to its title, simply 'Fontaines'. A reg-ular stone wall is punctuated by a sparse row of brass plaques which on closer inspection reveal themselves as taps. From one of these, in this unaccountably alarming picture, a young woman is filling a small, Virgin-shaped bottle. On the wall on which she leans, four more of these receptacles balance in miniature repetition of the apparition itself. But what holds me in this image is the woman herself: photographed from behind, the slim-mest expanse of her face is visible; her thick dark hair and pale blue cardigan are, according to a hallucinatory certainty which I know to be illusory but which grips me tighter the longer I look at this photo, those of my mother. To be precise, these details are exactly those of a photograph of my mother taken in the early 1960s.

She is photographed at the right-hand edge of a group of young women (they are perhaps the friends with whom she shared a flat before she married a few years later). As ever, she addresses the camera somewhat less directly, though more self-assuredly, than her companions. Like the woman in the slide, she wears a dark skirt and a pale blue top: both women have pushed their sleeves back to reveal a thin golden watch strap. The woman in the slide is not my mother and yet, as if for the first time, the congruence of dress, coiffure and jewellery situates my mother, the woman in this photograph I have looked at so many times, in another, unexpected place. The longer I compare these two images, the more I am convinced, despite myself, that they are exact contemporaries, that what I am seeing is the miraculous apparition of my mother at the shrine at Lourdes: a place I am sure she did not visit till at least a decade later. It is the strangest sort of anachronism: my mother, as a young woman, transported into her own future. For a moment I am convinced that on the sideboard behind my mother (my real mother) there must be some clue to this journey which I know she has not made. I have examined this photograph – and another taken minutes earlier or later – and although the background of this very ordinary 1960s interior is scattered with several mementoes, some of them clearly of a pious nature (a card depicting a Madonna and child, a calendar pinned to the wall which shows a robed figure who might be the Pope), I can find no trace of a visit to Lourdes. In sum, the coincidence affirms nothing, but persists in its curious attraction of the two disparate images into the same space: that of a memory I do not possess but have imagined countless times.

The shrine at Lourdes is there, however, in a photograph taken around the same time, in which my mother and one of her sisters (who looks ill at ease in her horn-rimmed glasses and new suit, as if she has just followed my mother to the city) appear alongside two older women whom I cannot identify. The room is old-fashioned, even slightly dingy: a dark smudge along the pale brownish wall connects the group at the centre of the picture to the edge of the frame. On a table behind and to the left of them, a small stack of what might be prayer books partially obscures a 'Child of Prague' identical to the plaster figure whose nocturnal migration I had once found so disturbing. But the detail I have never noticed until now, and which unexpectedly links this image of my mother to her later hopes of a miraculous intervention, is to be found on the wall, a few inches to the right of my mother's head. Framed in pale wood (on which an illegible inscription encloses the whole image) is a representation of rolling countryside and rising masonry which can only be a view of the Lourdes basilica. The church is unmistakable, with its central spire and two smaller, flanking towers. It stands isolated at the centre of a crudely montaged landscape. The town itself has been excised completely. (In a photograph from the slide album, taken from the same vantage point, the photographer has done nothing to crop out of view the several tall buildings to the left, nor to pretend that the basilica itself is unconnected, by at least three radiating roads or pathways, to the further buildings in the foreground.) Above and to the right of the basilica, thickly outlined in white, are two abutting arches, one twice the height of its neighbour. Here, hovering high over Lourdes and its environs, are the kneeling figure of Bernadette herself and, towering above her, the famed apparition – a thin streak of blue and white – that has drawn pilgrims to this spot for a century and a half.

This is not the last link in the chain of images and objects which leads me back from my memory of my mother's trips to Lourdes to the past significance of the town for my family. I had always imagined that Lourdes was a part only of my mother's set of personal and religious emblems. It was tied to her illness, to the sense that her faith in its consoling iconography and her real hope of finding a cure there had been passed on in the course of her own family's history of pilgrimage and prayer. I had not expected to find that it meant anything to my father; in fact I would have said that he viewed such traditional aspects of Irish Catholicism with some scepticism. His religious faith always seemed more bound up with private contemplation than public and communal displays of belief or hope. I could not have predicted that I should one day, while going though the few papers of his that I still possess, come across a second poem of his: a text which suggests that at some point the shrine at Lourdes was as significant for him as for my mother. The three stanzas appear to have been typed with the same typewriter as the poem devoted to the sinking of the *Red Bank* in 1969. The same yellowing paper bears my father's name at the bottom right-hand corner. The poem, which is, it turns out, also a prayer, is simply entitled 'Our Lady of Lourdes'. As a poem, it is, if anything, even less stylistically ambitious than the other. I might instead have said that it is less accomplished, but I realize I have no way of knowing what effect my father was after here. The first stanza sets a tone so plainly and uninflectedly pious that I can scarcely imagine he had anything in mind beyond an unadorned expression of devotion to the shrine and its luminous visitor: 'Bernadette Soubirous, / Handmaid of Mary. / Frail link with love divine / Seek balm for our healing. / Immaculate Conception / Be thou our Salvation.' The lines are addressed first to Bernadette and then to Mary; the second and third stanzas deploy what I cannot help but read as a series of dismaying clichés: 'still silence enfolds thee'; 'firm faith upholds thee'; 'Penance and prayer thy will, Our Highway to glory'. The thing is barely a poem at all, merely a rehearsal of devout convention. But it conjures for me now a level of belief I had not guessed at. I cannot conjecture that it means my father would also, as

243

my mother set out for Lourdes, have hoped for the sort of intervention the place promised. There are no miracles in my father's poem, and the 'healing' it imagines, I suspect, is more of the order of consolation than dramatic cure. But the poem connects him to my mother's increasing desperation in ways I never suspected. For that reason, and although it risks no clear personal investment in the set of pious images it describes, it strikes me as more human, more subjective than his somewhat cold poetic response to the tragedy that took place in Galway Bay a few weeks after I was born.

¶ *Seashore*

Ballyheigue Beside the Sea is the title of a slim little book, thirty-two pages in extent, with which as a child I used to renew my acquaintance every summer. I remember that a copy of it sat on a window sill of my grandfather's house, its jade-green cover faded by sunlight at the edges, but still vivid under the sturdier volumes from beneath which my brothers and I retrieved it each summer. Perhaps we were annually amazed to discover that the place that was so much a part of our own family holidays had a history deserving of record in a book. Copies of the book itself turned up, during the three weeks we spent each year near my mother's birthplace in Kerry, all over the village: prominently displayed in the gloomy little post office, tucked beside the tills of several shops. We may even have owned a copy, though I have no recollection of actually seeing it at home in Dublin. It was part of the texture of our holiday, as unchanging as the coastline and the single street that led from the beach through the village to a shrine to the Virgin Mary at the top: a sort of provincial replica of Lourdes, complete with artificial grotto but quite lacking a history of apparitions. Instead, as the book records, it was said that two women, late for Mass at the church further out of the village, had once been amazed to discover that from this spot they could, miraculously, hear every word the priest intoned, two miles away.

The copy of this book that I have recently acquired, and that sits before me now, has a bright orange cover which informs me that it is the third edition; it is, however, undated, and I have no way of knowing how long after my last visit to Ballyheigue it might have been printed (I have disallowed the unlikely possibility that this well-preserved copy predates my own acquaintance with the place). Between the title and the name of the local author – Joseph Moriarty, whom I now recall as the village postmaster – a rather cursory line drawing depicts a family group on the seashore: a scene in which I used to discern at the extreme right the outline of the cliffs that ran west from the village, here declining sharply to the horizon I imagined denoted the place where my mother was born and grew up. Even now, if I gaze long enough at this roughly delineated coast-line, I can trace the long walk out of the village and along the cliff-top, then up the steep boreen to the farm which was once my grandfather's and which belonged, in the time I knew it, to one of my mother's two brothers (he died the summer before her). The name of that place – Ballylongane – appears on the first page of the book, along with the names of twenty-three other townlands that surround the village proper, and I realize that I have never before seen that name written or printed and could not, until now, have ventured to spell it (as a child, I couldn't even pronounce it, so impenetrable was the tangle of vowels and guessed-at consonants that I heard and consequently avoided attempting to replicate). I realize too that I must never actually have read this book, such is the profusion of legend that attaches to a village I have for years only recalled as framing the events of one particular summer. Of this history, I had only the dimmest knowledge. If I try to map the significant points in the topography surrounding my childhood memories of the place, they fit unexpectedly the contours of Joseph Moriarty's account. I recall certain details of which I was sure as a child but which turn out to have been only half comprehended. I have had it in my head for the best part of three decades that a fleeing ship of the Spanish Armada had been wrecked on the rocks just west of the village, its crew lured to the castle above, poisoned, and the ship's treasures stolen. The real nautical adventure for which the village is known turns out to be both more historically significant and just as melodramatic.

On 21 April, Good Friday, 1916, at around half past two in the morning, Roger Casement and two companions left a German U-boat out in the bay. Their small boat capsized and they swam ashore. Later, from prison, Casement wrote to his sister:

> When I landed in Ireland that morning, swamped and swimming ashore on an unknown strand I was happy for the first time for over a year. Although I knew that this fate waited on me, I was for one brief spell happy and smiling once more. I cannot tell you what I felt. The sandhills were full of skylarks, rising in the dawn, the first I had heard for years – the first sound I heard through the surf was their song as I waded in through the breakers, and they kept rising all the time up to the old rath at Currahane [sic] ... and all round were primroses and wild violets and the singing of the sky-larks in the air, and I was back in Ireland again.

Casement had fetched up at Banna Strand, just south of the village of Ballyheigue itself. Shortly after midnight, one James Moriarty (what relation, if any, to the author of the book in front of me, I do not know) had been checking his rabbit traps when he saw the submarine's signal lights, but had no idea what he was looking at. Other locals spied three men on the road by the shore in the early morning, the abandoned boat and a cache of arms buried in the sand. None of this appears in Joseph Moriarty's brief history of his village; nor was the story ever recounted in my hearing during the weeks (amounting to a total of a year, I calculate) I spent in Ballyheigue, though it was still certainly within living memory, not least that of my grandfather. I do not even recall the erection of a statue of Casement in the summer of 1984. Perhaps the events that followed immediately on Casement's coming ashore had buried the tale till all who might have something to lose by its telling were dead. Casement had quickly been arrested, and plans by the local volunteers to spring him from the barracks at Tralee, 12 miles from Ballyheigue, came to nothing; such a daring raid would doubtless have risked revealing the secret of the coming rising. In all, Casement spent thirty-one hours in Kerry; accounts of the event note that he came ashore at Banna Strand, but often elide the existence of the two villages whose occupants played a part in the drama: Ballyheigue at one end of the beach, Ardfert a few miles away at the other.

In the time I knew it, Ballyheigue was first of all a thriving holiday destination, then a rapidly fading relic of domestic tourism in a period when foreign holidays became the norm for many. Postcards from the 1970s, picturing the resort as idyllically remote, show a beach and village that are barely inhabited; within a decade they would actually start to look like this again. In the usual lurid view, courtesy of the John Hinde Studio, a couple of tiny colourful figures interrupt the blazing whiteness of the empty seashore. The reality, by the time I dashed excitedly down the same slope to the water, was rather different: in the mid-seventies, the long beach would have been thickly dotted for several hundred yards with holidaymakers. We always walked to the far end of the throng to find a secluded spot a little way back from the beach, where, in among the sand dunes, you could still imagine that the strand (it was never a 'beach' to us) was a secret, as it had been when my mother must have walked it as a child. Here, one was shielded even from the noise of the seashore: a tumult that would hit you again, like a gust of warm air, as you reached the top of a high dune and contemplated (but not for too long, in case you should lose your nerve) a spectacular leap back down to the populous foreshore. By the early eighties, the crowds had begun to thin out, and from the summer my mother died, I have no recollection at all of the hordes that once made of Ballyheigue a place of magical ease and garish busyness. It seemed, that summer, already to have outlived its meaning as part of the landscape of my childhood.

¶ Sea view

The village, which has left me with so many clear and cherished memories of childhood holidays, seems to vanish entirely when I think of the summer of 1985. Our last family holiday, I remember, was already uncertain, and organized by my father at the last minute in the midst of the chaos that surrounded my mother's failing health. Only weeks earlier, she had had the nail of one index finger removed, as the circulation to her hands was now so restricted, and the skin so badly damaged, that she was threatened with gangrene. The pain that racked her whole body now focussed itself to this excruciating point: her hand bandaged and held awkwardly as she sank into her seat on the train and closed her eyes. The day before we left, she and my father had been to see the specialist who, years before, had admitted that the symptoms of her disease were the worst he had seen, and I knew from my parents' silence on the subject that something had been revealed at that meeting, something other than the visible maiming of her body had been discussed, a secret that lurked unacknowledged in the silence of that long journey. I remember my distinct feeling that the world had further closed around us, that as I looked out at a landscape which seemed distant and laminated, I was looking for the last time at a world falling away as swiftly as the train sped through the countryside.

For the second consecutive summer, my father had rented a house on a hill above the village, some distance from the modest chalets, closer to the seafront, where we usually stayed. We were cut off from the bustle of other holidaymakers, and I don't think that adolescence alone can explain the sense I had, that previous summer, that our annual routine was at an end. I recall only two moments from that holiday: the sound of a carnival in the village below, its music drifting across the fields from a distance my glum teenage imagination had already sentimentally consigned to the past; and hours spent sitting, reading, before a large picture window which gave out on to a dismally wet summer I was content to accord with my new attitude of universal boredom. But my separation of myself from the scene of the family holiday may not have been entirely selfish: there was already something deathly about that house, perched windily, adjacent to the village's ancient, long disused graveyard.

I don't know how long we had been in the house before I realized that my mother was dying, but I recall the instant distinctly. She had left the house only once. I remember her dismay on discovering that it was the only accommodation available; she could no longer walk back up the hill from the village, and so was trapped. She spent most of our first days there in bed, until her sister arrived (I know now why she was there: her husband and children had returned to Dublin the previous week) and drove her the few hundred yards to the seafront. She had not been able to get out of the car. That evening, as we sat down to dinner, my aunt tried to console her; she had at least got out of the house, had seen something of her home village despite everything. But my mother, as I recall, remained silent on that subject. All I remember of the meal – during which she ate nothing – is that she tried to describe the pain she was in, and that (I am least certain of this detail, perhaps because I had heard her say it so often) she said she was dying. In any case, I was sure of it: I knew that the brief time she had spent looking out at a rainswept shore was the last opportunity she would have to look at that view.

It was not yet dawn when I woke the following morning; my father came into the room where my eldest brother and I were sleeping to tell us that an ambulance was on its way. My mother had not slept, and in the early morning had told my father that she felt as though she could not wait till daybreak. There was no need yet, he said, for us to get up. I lay there picturing the ambulance leaving the town, 12 miles away, and wondered if it would arrive in time. I wondered too if my brothers knew what I had already guessed (we said nothing as we waited), and I hoped for an instant that whatever was to come would be over quickly. In the following days, as my mother drifted in and out of consciousness, and the house filled with relatives while my father spent most of the day at her bedside, I became convinced that if she died, that split second in which I wished for a swift end would have sealed her fate. My mother, we were told a couple of days later, was improving, and although she had asked for us, we were not taken to see her. In fact, we hardly moved from the house at all, so that the week we spent waiting for her to be declared stable enough to be moved to a Dublin hospital now seems to have unfolded entirely within the walls of that house, as if it were connected to the (for me, almost imaginary) hospital and had drifted away from the surrounding landscape, the seashore, the waves which continued to beat against the concrete promontory that had been the scene of my mother's last glimpse of the outside world. I wonder if that image might have joined the picture of her three sons in her mind as it battled with a certainty that, in her waking moments, I have no doubt my father tried to dispel.

Is it too beguiling a thought, too obviously a product of the mourner's retrospective construction of consoling symmetries, to imagine that she had kept the worst at bay until she had seen this view? I remember that my father and I had taken a walk along the beach during that week. In my memory, we walk silently for miles, all the way to a point just inland of a small island known as the Black Rock, to which, at low tide, we had often made our way and looked back at the beach, the village, the cliffs curving away, retreating behind huge expanses of rock where my mother had played as a child. A few days later, after my father had returned from a visit to the hospital, he asked me to accompany him on another walk, around the outskirts of the village. It was pouring rain, and as we came back along the main street he suggested we stop for a while at the village's only hotel. As we sat in the darkness of the deserted bar, my father told me as much as he could about my mother's condition. When we got home, he said, we would have to watch her; she would still be very ill. He did not quite say (how could he have said this?) that she was going to die, but simply that she would not get any better. I understood, and immediately imagined that I would be the one to find her dead. I was sure she would not die until we were all back in Dublin. I pictured the house in Dublin empty but for my mother and myself (imagining, despite everything, an ordinary afternoon: my father at work, my brothers out for the day). I would come in to the kitchen to find her lying at my feet. I pictured, in other words, a return to a minimal sort of normality, for a matter of weeks at least. I thought I would have time to let the certainty of my mother's death separate me further from the outside world. And once again, I felt ashamed.

On 16 July 1985, my brothers and I travelled home from Kerry by train, my father having left earlier that morning in the ambulance that took my mother to a hospital in Dublin. Her condition was sufficiently stable for her to be moved, but also grave enough for the staff of the hospital in Kerry to know that they could do nothing further for her. I recall that as I sat on that train pretending to read, I imagined the ambulance tracing its different route across the country, passing through the same towns and perhaps even reaching them on occasion at the same time. I wondered whether the ambulance would stop somewhere along the way, and if so whether there were arrangements for such a break in its journey. I imagined, as we sped airlocked in our own rapidly thickening atmosphere of dread, my parents as a sort of satellite to our orbit round whatever it was that was about to occur, whatever awaited us in a place, our home, that I could now hardly remember. It was not a journey I wanted to complete, because at the end of it we would emerge into a newly and fearfully dilated air, and somehow the chamber in which my family had been secluded for several days had come to seem weirdly comfortable, as if we might have carried on in that way for months.

We reached the station in the early evening; an aunt and uncle were waiting to take us home. As the car moved slowly through the city, I remembered the past childhood summers when we had taken this journey by taxi, and my father's predictable question (carried on, with cheerful sarcasm, till we were far too old), as we passed along the river and into the centre of town: 'Do you know where you are yet?' It was a route that always took us past the psychiatric hospital to which, over the years, I had accompanied my mother so many times. On this last journey, I realized that I had never, as a child, understood the distinctions between the various hospitals my mother had attended. It was only in the last year of her life that I fully acknowledged that the walk up from the brooding stone-pillared gates to this hospital, and back down again, stopping at a dispensary just inside the gates for my mother to collect her medication, was connected to the depression she had suffered for a decade or more. I have completely eradicated its interior from my memory: only these two short journeys, separated each time by a waiting room of which I recall nothing, remain to convince me that I did actually go with her on her visits to her psychiatrist. To me, it was just another hospital; the bus trips (this one, I recall, involved two) punctuated the mid-afternoons when I returned from primary school and regularly interrupted my summer holidays without causing me much unease. It was later, when my brothers and I were old enough to stay at home, that I came to understand these excursions and, though still dimly, to fear my mother's return and the next diagnosis or development of her treatment.

There were, over the years, many hospital visits, but I have only one very clear memory of the hospital where my mother's scleroderma was treated and where she spent, as the disease progressed, more and more time. I remember only vaguely the waiting room where my brothers and I were left as my father was taken to her ward, and how eventually he would reappear to lead us in to see her. On this particular occasion, my mother came downstairs with him, and I have never forgotten my panic as she came slowly down the huge staircase and round into the lobby. As I stood up in the waiting room, surrounded by families warmly greeting their sick relatives, or embracing as they said goodbye, I discovered that I had strictly no notion of how to behave. I could not imagine that my mother was about to kiss me or put her arms round me: would this intimacy, unknown since infancy, suddenly connect me to a suffering body I had come to think of as quite distant, secluded in the bed of the ward from which she had just emerged? The thought was unbearable, and I wonder now if she felt it too; the way her illness had cut her off from a natural contact with the children standing in front of her, shuffling, uncomfortable, shamed. It may have been after that particular visit that I came to fear the building itself. I no longer dared look at the patients around my mother, nor risk a glance through the open doors of the wards I passed on the way to hers. I ceased to think of a hospital as a place where you went to be cured; now it was a place dedicated to humiliation and degradation, a place where nameless forces sucked one in and thrust one out again looking weaker, less like oneself. The place became, as I got stuck in this childish perception, my most extreme metaphor of the inexplicable history that was unfolding around me.

My mother and father were both buried in the large cemetery not far from our house. Originally the site of the residence of the Shaw family, owners of Bushy Park, a few miles away to the south, Mount Jerome cemetery was constituted by an Act of Parliament in 1837, and entrusted to the General Cemetery Company of Dublin, which ran it till the company was liquidated late in 1984. I remember that when my grandfather died in December of that year, there was some doubt about the future of Mount Jerome, but it seems that by the following summer it had been purchased by a large firm of undertakers and there was no question but that my mother would be buried there. I knew the cemetery well. My father's mother had been buried there in the autumn of 1974, and visits to her grave were a regular feature of the Sunday afternoons of my childhood. I had always been fascinated by the older, original parts of the site. I knew that the earliest grave dated from 1837, and my brothers and I would sometimes wander off, as my parents went to fetch water for the flowers they had bought at a small shop just outside the massive green iron gates, to search for this ancient tomb. We never found it, but were often thrilled to discover, each time, an even older grave than we had last time. The original 25-acre cemetery had expanded westwards to take up 45 acres, surrounded by suburban houses. The point where the old cemetery ended and the new began, I imagined, was marked by the sudden cessation of the avenues of yews which grew there. We had to walk along the longest of these to reach my grandmother's grave, and I never ceased to be thrilled by the decaying stonework of the huge nineteenth-century tombs I found on either side. As you neared the turn-off to an open, unlandscaped expanse, the monuments became suddenly less exciting. They lacked the ravaged or headless angels, battered urns or – as in at least one case – faithful stone dogs which marked the plots of defunct Victorians whose bones, I imagined, I might one day catch sight of, if only their graves would subside another few inches. As my parents coaxed me along towards my grandmother's grave, I often longed to turn back and explore the sunken pathways that radiated from a towering mock-Gothic chapel passed by on the way in. There, I knew, if one happened on the right rusted doorway, a thick white lattice at the top would allow just enough light to see inside. There, piled up on both sides in the gloom, would be the huge lead coffins which were the grim sight I was after.

My parents' grave is off to one side of the path along which I was dragged as a child. Unlike my grandparents' plot further off into the open and wind-whipped area where marble headstones and golden letters predominate (surrounded by the crunch of variously coloured chippings), this spot still feels as if it is part of the old cemetery. But the graves on the side of this narrow, muddy path have been jammed against a dismal grey wall. On the other side is a stonemason's yard, where blank headstones stand in serried ranks awaiting their names and legends. My parents' grave, from a distance, is hardly visible. I recall that my father had wanted the plainest of headstones; I remember him refusing all suggestions of gilt lettering and solid ornament. A simple flat stone comes to a bare point above two inscriptions that could hardly be more modest: apart from the names and dates, the headstone records only 'a dear wife and mother' and 'dear husband and father'. There is nothing of the elaborate versification that crowds the black marble of the grave on the left, nor any hint of an individuality I used always to find disturbing on my trips here as a child: those graves with photographs of the deceased attached were considerably more eerie than any of the Victorian extravagances.

I have in front of me a photograph of the grave. It reminds me that in the years since my father's death I have visited it just once, and then only after several years of putting the moment off time and again. But I have never stopped imagining it. In my memory it stayed freshly dug for years; then, as guilt over my abandoning it set in, I imagined it becoming overgrown until its inscription was scarcely legible. In fact, of course, it had stayed much as it appears in the photograph: pallid and unexceptional, a muted reminder, nothing to be afraid of. I cannot say that when, at last, I stood in front of it again, the grave lived up to the fears I had built up in the intervening years. I had thought there would be something unspeakable to face here: a reckoning with the past I had done my best to bury. The sight of the grave, I fancied, would return me to the state of inexpressible distress I felt every time my father took me there during the five years he survived my mother. Then, I would stand staring at the dull grey mass, wondering precisely what it was I was supposed to feel. It was this thought, rather than any access of grief, that so frightened me, and kept me from returning. The grave, I thought, would be an accusation written in stone; its lack of embellishment or iconography would remind me of the silence that enclosed the two bodies that lay there. I had been unable to express my fear of this place, or of the memories that were dispersed about this particular damp and colourless corner of the cemetery. But when I stood before the grave for the first time in a decade, it seemed as if it had sunk into itself to such a degree, become so much a part of the lifelessness of its surroundings, that it no longer said anything to me.

CODA

'What we need is silence; but what silence requires
is that I go on talking.'
— John Cage, *Silence*

The silence that wrapped itself around my memories of my parents is soundtracked, in my mind, by the music that emanated, for a decade or so, from a corner of our sitting room. My brothers and I seem to have used music to address, obscurely or otherwise, the absences at the heart of our household. Music stood in, endlessly, for all that we would not or could not say.

The record player in the corner of the room was a Pye Playboy that dated, I suppose, from sometime in the 1960s. Perhaps my parents had bought or been given it when they married towards the end of the decade. It was a rather archaic-looking object, built solidly of wood and, if at all datable in its quite graceless lines, more plausibly a relic of the 1940s. When I was very young, my mother would regularly, mid-afternoon, take out one of the handful of records she owned – a fairly predictable selection of Irish folk standards and their more recent imitations – and either play along on her newly acquired guitar, or set two of the three of us dancing in front of her. (In my memory, Kevin is still a tiny bundle at the other side of the room.) Music must have leached away from my mother's life over the years – as her hands had curled too tightly to shape a chord on the guitar, or as depression sapped her energy for dancing. In any case, there was a gap of several years, as I recall, between these joyful, childish sessions and the time when the record player came back to life: first as I started to play my own records, then as my brothers began to compete for the turntable. The thing itself was remarkably sturdy; its single speaker was capable of startling loudness and its two controls (volume and tone) never failed for at least twenty years. With some careful adjustment and a little optimism, it could still be made to play in the late 1990s.

My father's contribution to my parents' small record

collection comprised a few old 78s of light classical music: waltzes, light opera. For all I knew, he might well have shown more enthusiasm as a young man, when these recordings were current, but my memory of him suggests that my father was actually afraid of music. It was as though he suspected that if he allowed too extreme (too beautiful, too austere, too languid or frenetic) a sound to touch him, his sense of self-possession might unravel. He had, if pushed, his favourites; but these choices were so lacking in pretension, so unadventurous even for a middle-aged man of steady temperament and distracting cares, that he might as well not have bothered. I discovered in my teens that his lack of interest in music had made him usefully impervious to the trashiest sounds to which I could expose him. He greeted everything with the same weary scorn. I sometimes tried to penetrate his shell of sarcasm and indifference, but could never hit on the right frequency to startle or soften his disregard. It was not even a matter of genre: there were times, I'm sure, when I tried to trick him with an uncharacteristic classical piece, yet provoked not the slightest response.

I think I know now what I was trying to achieve. After my mother died, in 1985, the enthusiasm my brothers and I already shared (though we had few tastes in common) turned swiftly to obsession. Of course, I can only test my own preoccupation against those of my contemporaries, but eventually even friends with whom I had discussed certain key discoveries (my own canon was constructed of extremes of pure, disposable pop and wilful, noisy obscurity) began to tire of my inability to think or talk about anything else. But it wasn't a community I was after. I had never had a sense to start with that music was something to be shared: my passion was monomaniacal and, when it came to talking about it, monologic too. I still cannot quite grasp what people mean when they say that the music of their adolescence reminds them of a specific moment: a season, a milieu, a romance. I recall only the time spent actively listening. Music was never a backdrop to anything else; it was the central (for a long time the only) drama, the sole nexus of interest and energy in my life, so much so that I now wonder what it was I was trying to hear, or not to hear. I remember the first record I bought after my mother died, and how, at the end of a month during which I had hardly left the house, I had been seized by this extraordinary song, fleetingly heard on television: a sort of hymn to preternatural weather, a giddy, soaring three minutes of strangeness and fragility. (Or so it still sounds to me; were I to name it, it might mean nothing, or far too much.) Scared that my sudden access of interest in the outside world was as yet inadmissible, I had to smuggle into the house the 7-inch single I bought a few days later and hide it, hoping I could listen to it later without disturbing the silence that had persisted there since my mother's death. In the end, it proved impossible: I had to play it, that evening, with my father and brothers in the room. I remember that I crouched, blushing, in the corner by the record player as a parade of synthesized strings and military drums gave way to a woman's voice so eloquently grief-stricken to my ears that I almost had to tear the record from the turntable, such was my discomposure. With my back to the rest of the room, I was unsure whether the song was going unnoticed or had actually, as I feared, opened and healed, in its brief span, a sort of wound in the air between us. The song seemed too unbearably tender a thing to have introduced into the room; I resolved to listen to it only when I was alone.

264

Over the next few years, and on into the time after my father died, music became a way of perpetuating and obscuring the silence, of not having to choose between silence and speech, of avoiding the subject and letting it vibrate in the atmosphere, translated into sound, a thousand times. We dreamed, I think, of a sound, of a song, that would say what we could not and that would at the same time excuse us from ever having to say anything. I can find no other way of explaining what happened in those final years in the house, when music was a way for my brothers and me to avoid speaking to one another: sometimes comically so, as when we would try to drown out one another's voices by simply turning up the volume. Our competing record collections became weapons in an undeclared war of musical sensibilities which were really something else: our incompatible responses to our predicament. And yet music was also what we shared, sometimes the only thing we might admit to sharing, the only arena in which any emotional currency other than rage was exchanged.

I have sometimes wondered whether that combination of silence and noise is what has caused me to forget completely what my parents' voices sounded like. I can remember songs, not listened to since, better than I can recall the voices of my parents as I last heard them. I certainly look like my father; but do I sound like him? To my ear, numerous tiny cues in my own voice sound as if they have come from my father's; but I have only to listen to the recorded sound of my voice – thin, inauthentic, immature – for the impression to disappear.

Although I cannot hear my parents' voices, I hear myself talking to them all the time, and only ever in anger. I am forced to imagine what it is like to be an adult whose parents are living, and so I have little notion what emotional accommodations are called for on either side in order to arrive (if indeed this is what happens) at a kind of equilibrium. In my daydreams, my parents stay silent while I carry on talking: admonishing, complaining, settling countless tiny scores. Or I simply rehearse arguments I did actually have (especially with my father); this time, I win. These are not traumatic flashbacks, but rather, I think, pretences on which to return to the house (we are always in the sitting room, from which I imagine the rest of the house hovering out of sight above me) and to hear, faintly at first, then rising to compete with my own voice, and finally drowning it out altogether, an imagined song. The song seems to come from nowhere specific within the house, but to drift up out of the foundations, to set the whole house vibrating, to fill the empty rooms around me, to be at once every song that was played to keep those rooms from pressing too hard upon us and the sound of escape, of air rushing through a house that has been allowed to breathe at last. It is the song we were searching for and it says, for the first time, because nobody has had the strength to say it before, that something is missing.

Readings

Theodor Adorno, *Minima Moralia*, trans. E. F. N. Jephcott (London, Verso, 1994).

Giorgio Agamben, *The Man Without Content*, trans. Georgia Albert (Stanford, Stanford University Press, 1999).

St Augustine, *Confessions*, trans. F. J. Sheed (Indianapolis, Hackett, 1993).

Gaston Bachelard, *The Poetics of Space*, trans. Maria Jolas (Boston, Beacon Press, 1994).

Roland Barthes, *Camera Lucida*, trans. Richard Howard (London, Fontana, 1990).

Geoffrey Batchen, *Forget Me Not: Photography and Remembrance* (New York, Princeton Architectural Press, 2004).

Charles Baudelaire, *Selected Writings on Art and Literature*, trans. P. E. Charvet (London, Penguin, 1993).

Walter Benjamin, *Selected Writings, Volume 3*, trans. Edmund Jephcott et al. (Cambridge, Mass., Harvard University Press, 2002).

John Berger and Jean Mohr, *A Fortunate Man* (New York, Pantheon, 1976).

Henri Bergson, *Matter and Memory*, trans. N. M. Paul and W. Scott Palmer (London, Swan Sonnenschein, 1911).

Jorge Luis Borges, *Labyrinths*, trans. Donald A. Yates and James E. Irby (London, Penguin, 1970).

Joe Brainard, *I Remember* (New York, Penguin, 1995).

Sir Thomas Browne, *The Major Works* (Harmondsworth, Penguin, 1977).

John Cage, *Silence* (Middletown, Wesleyan University Press, 1961).

E. M. Cioran, *A Short History of Decay*, trans. Richard Howard (New York, Arcade Publishing, 1998).

Steven Connor, *The Book of Skin* (London, Reaktion, 2004).

Thomas De Quincey, *Confessions of an English Opium-Eater* (London, Macdonald, 1956).

Tacita Dean, *Seven Books* (Göttingen, Steidl, 2003).

Charles Dickens, *David Copperfield* (London, Penguin, 1996).

Georges Didi-Huberman, *Invention of Hysteria: Charcot and the Photographic Iconography of the Salpêtrière*, trans. Alisa Hartz (Cambridge, Mass., MIT Press, 2003).

John Donne, *The Major Works* (Oxford, Oxford University Press, 1990).

George Eliot, *Middlemarch* (London, Penguin, 2003).

Ruth Harris, *Lourdes: Body and Spirit in the Secular Age* (New York, Viking, 1999).

Gabriel Josipovici, *Touch* (New Haven, Yale University Press, 1996).

Jacques Henri Lartigue, *Lartigue: Album of a Century*, ed. Martine d'Astier et al. (London, Hayward Gallery, 2004).

Chris Marker, *La Jetée: ciné-roman* (New York, Zone Books, 1992).

Vladimir Nabokov, *Speak, Memory: An Autobiography Revisited* (Harmondsworth, Penguin, 1982).

Celeste Olalquiaga, *The Artificial Kingdom: A Treasury of the Kitsch Experience* (London, Bloomsbury, 1999).

Georges Perec, *Species of Spaces and Other Pieces*, trans. John Sturrock (London, Penguin, 1998).

Marcel Proust, *Remembrance of Things Past*, trans. C. K. Scott Moncrieff and Terence Kilmartin (London, Penguin, 1989).

August Sander, *People of the Twentieth Century* (New York, Harry N. Abrams, 2002).

W. G. Sebald and Jan Peter Tripp, *Unrecounted*, trans. Michael Hamburger (London, Hamish Hamilton, 2004).

Rebecca Solnit, *Wanderlust: A History of Walking* (London, Verso, 2001).

Rachel Whiteread, *House* (London, Phaidon, 1995).

Virginia Woolf, *To the Lighthouse* (London, Grafton, 1977).

Frances Yates, *The Art of Memory* (London, Pimlico, 1994).

Fitzcarraldo Editions
8-12 Creekside
London, SE8 3DX
United Kingdom

ISBN 978-1910695-72-2

Design by Ray O'Meara
Typeset in Fitzcarraldo
Printed and bound by TJ Books

fitzcarraldoeditions.com

Fitzcarraldo Editions